ATONEMENT

D0907517

ATONEMENT

The Million Man March

Edited by Kim Martin Sadler

The Pilgrim Press

Cleveland, Ohio

The Pilgrim Press, Cleveland, Ohio 44115
© 1996 by The Pilgrim Press

01 00 99 98 97 96   5 4 3 2 1

Library of Congress Cataloging-in-Publication Data

Atonement : the Million Man March / edited by Kim Martin Sadler.
     p.   cm.
  ISBN 0–8298–1147–8 (acid-free paper)
  1. Million Man March, Washington, D.C., 1995. 2. Afro-American men—Conduct of life. I. Sadler, Kim Martin.
F201.A86   1996
305.38'896073—dc20   96–34327
                                  CIP

IN MEMORIAM

The Scottsboro Boys, Black Zeek, Harry Moore, James Powell, Emmett Till, Yusef Hawkins, Charles Lang, Ernest Green, Collins Mondon, Phillip Morton Peddie, Charles Kimble, Johnny Kimble, "White Mike," Edward C. Neale Jr., Alexander "Boobie" Eldridge, Derek Claiborne, Ricky Sewer, LaKeith Russell, "Pistol Pete," "Gangster Lenny," Trent, Al Plowden, Jerry Martin, Alvin Johnson, Gus Moorehead, Ron Croxton, Richard Blount Jr., Jeffrey Bell, Father Curtis Sisco, David Daniels, Anthony Steele, William Carrington, Michael Boone, Nathan Leach, Zarick Clegg, H. Kirk Harris, Mr. Moses, Mr. Applewhite, Mr. Brooks, Mr. White, Mr. Lawrence, Mr. Thornton, Samuel "Pop Pop" Sadler Sr., Joseph "Poppa" Goodwin, and Jesse Frierson III

CONTENTS

Foreword   *Michael Eric Dyson*   xi

Introduction   xv

Excerpts: From a Black Woman to a Black Man   xvi
   Maya Angelou

The Million Man March Pledge   xvii

REFLECTIONS

A View from a Hill   *Ronald S. Bonner Sr.*   3

The March before the March   *Shawn M. Barney*   5

What Happens When No One Comes?   *Richard M. Bundy Jr.*   8

Enough to Make a Difference   *Thomas E. Wortham III*   13

Gays and the Million Man March   *Keith Boykin*   16

A Religious Experience   *Jeremiah A. Wright Jr.*   18

I Want to Be in That Number   *Nathan Warren Reed*   22

No Ordinary Day   *Neil James Bullock*   26

The Choice   *Alex Pickens Jr.*   30

A Lesson Well Received   *Alex Pickens III*   32

Long Live the Spirit of the Million Man March   34
   Seth W. Pickens

A Family Reunion   *Martini Shaw*   36

Meeting the Challenge   *André P. Tramble*   37

A One-Time Experience   *Eric L. Hill*   41

What Did It Mean?   *Granville K. White*   43

Building a Network   *Steve H. Alexander*   45

The Message and the Messenger   *Anonymous*   49

The "Eyes" Have It   *Hugh Brandon*   50

Our Collective Responsibility   *Jack Sullivan Jr.*   52

We Owe Our Very Best   *Richard A. Rowe*   54

Something Happened   *Amoti Nyabongo*   57

Called Out   *Ronald Cook*   60

Seize the Time   *Silas Norman Jr.*   63

Poised for a Revolution   *Todd L. Ledbetter*   66

Unity of the Spirit   *Nathaniel Martin*   71

A Black Man Who Loves Black Men's Eyes   *Cleo Manago*   73

Voices of the Past   *Rodney Franklin*   77

Phi Beta Sigma Answers the Call!   *Lawrence E. Miller*   79

A Day That Would Not Turn Me Loose!   80
   Wendell Harrison Fitzgerald Phillips

One for All and All for One   *F. Allison Phillips*   84

Imagine Our New Greatness   *Douglas S. Lee*   86

The Power of the Message   *David P. Gardner*   88

Countering the Conspiracy   *Jawanza Kunjufu*   90

The Trumpet Sounds   *Paul S. Burley*   92

A Sweet Spirit   *Howard Brookins Sr.*   95

The Goal Was Accomplished   *Howard B. Brookins Jr.*   97

Umoja!   *Lawrence Oliver Hall*   99

Guidance from My Sisters   *Carl K. Harmon*   101

The Long Arm of History   *Austin J. Dunn Jr.*   104

Called by God   *Morris Allen Jr.*   106

Thousands upon Thousands   *David B. Miller*   108

Our Wounds Are Deep   *Larry Grant Coleman*   110

A Little Brother's Request   *Larry Grant Coleman*   112

An Astounding Assignment   *Ben Holbert*   115

The Clarion Call   *Wardell J. Payne*   117

One in a Million   *James Raymond Reid*   120

Symbol to Substance: Where Do We Go from Here?   123
   Monte E. Norwood

Rise into Flight   *Morgan Burton Jr.*   127

The Day We Witnessed Our Potential   *Craig A. Thompson*   128

Strengthening One Generation at a Time   *Wayne L. Wilson*   130

The Million Man March: A Sermon for Discussion   133
  Frank A. Thomas

SPEECHES

It's a Brothers' Thing   *Conrad W. Worrill*   141

Greetings   *Rosa Parks*   143

Up, You Mighty People   *Queen Mother Moore*   144

Resources   145

Contributors   147

FOREWORD

By almost any measure, the Million Man March was a historic and monumental achievement for African Americans. It grew out of the desperate need to confront the agonies of Black men. How we are often unjustly perceived and treated in American society. How we frequently turn with vicious abandon on one another, and our families, in word and deed.

The Million Man March sought to raise the visions and hopes of Black men. Black men from every class and nearly every county in our nation converged on Washington to boldly testify to our desire to make right what had gone wrong. In our relationships with our wives, daughters, lovers, nieces, stepdaughters, aunts, mothers, and grandmothers. In our relationships with our sons, brothers, nephews, stepsons, uncles, fathers, and grandfathers.

We met there—brother to brother, man to man, soul to soul—to help one another bear the burdens and blessings of Black masculinity. Its secret joys. Its hidden hopes. Its frustrated quests. Its prolonged journeys. Its untold heroism. Its unspoken terrors. Its disguised heartbreaks. Its uplifting aspirations. Its painful fears. And in the end, its naked, raw, unmasked wish—as one of its most eloquent brothers phrased it during a time when racial suffering gave even our romantic longings a veiled, transcendent meaning—to love and be loved in return. Yes, Nat's desire became—if just for a moment, and if its boundaries are defined more by principle than pigment, more by common suffering than singular purpose, more by spirit than gender—a Black race's dream of lasting liberation.

From the very beginning, the March faced difficulties and its own contradictions. Its ideals, its intentions, its inspiration, and surely its leadership were bathed in homegrown American controversy. We can classify much of the hullabaloo as the feverish moral passion too many White folk seem to stumble upon only when it is convenient—that is, when the cost for their ethical outrage doesn't involve structural changes to our nation's economy or politics. Or, as White response to the O. J. Simpson verdict proves, many White folk get outdone when Black behavior is contrary to White expectations. Still, we've got to admit that some of the criticism of the Million Man March was legitimate.

It's true, for instance, that Minister Louis Farrakhan—despite the dramatic fashion in which he drowns paranoid White fears, which feed on historical amnesia, in a nearly unfathomable ocean of Black memories of suffering—also speaks from a narrow and limiting religious orientation. And as is the case with all fundamentalists, his perspective is sometimes theologically rigid and often antidemocratic. Such beliefs and behavior are not endemic to Muslims; it's a tradition with which Baptists, Pentecostals, and, yes, even Catholics are intimately familiar. That's why homophobia runs rampant in our religious communities. That's why the gender apartheid of the Black church—where Black women, who constitute the majority of church members, are routinely closed out of formal priestly or pastoral power—is much more pernicious than the Nation of Islam's more obvious gender barriers.

This history of Black patriarchy is the reason so many Black feminists and gays and lesbians opposed with good reason the Million Man March. To them, it looked like yet another rush of testosterone for Black men. Another attempt, no matter how highfalutin it sounded, to secure stronger status in White America by getting the upper hand on "queers and women." Fortunately, the March, for the most part, put such fears to rest. The more than million Black men assembled that day were motivated by high moral purposes. To atone for our failures as Black men. To take greater responsibility for our own plight. To reconcile with Black women and one another in the fight for dignity and self-respect.

Louis Farrakhan's genius is that he recognized that Black men possess moral ambitions that are both higher and deeper than our nation has often been willing to credit us for. He understood that beneath the various hungers Black men have—for bread, justice, health, stability—the greatest of hungers is, after all, a spiritual one.

That doesn't play well with folk who've invested ultimate belief in strategies that are bound to time and dust. But for those of us who envision, however imperfectly, a world shaped from the indestructible forces of faith, hope, and love, the Million Man March is a pinnacle of spiritual inspiration. It continues to give breath and life to ideals that, before they materialize, many Black men dare not entertain.

With the action it may continue to ignite, the Million Man March can nurture liberating, self-critical Black men who will only rest when the weapons of destruction aimed at our lives—including those we have ourselves fashioned and wielded—can be reshaped into narratives that reflect our pain, that hold our potential as a people. The greatest virtue of this book—drawn from Black men who heard and saw for themselves, indeed who *made* for themselves the history that will be written about—is that it assembles so many honest and healing narratives. Drink them. Eat them. Meditate with them. Dispute them. Measure your hope against them. But don't—you simply can't—ignore them.

Michael Eric Dyson

INTRODUCTION

October 16, 1995, will find its place in the history of this nation as the day that African American men, one million strong, gathered in one place, in one spirit, and with one purpose: to atone. They gathered at the Million Man March to atone for the sins of the past and to commit to the progress of the future.

They came thousands upon thousands, as far as the eye could see, a vast ocean of men, African men, standing tall on the shoulders of Moses, Marcus, Martin, Malcolm, and Mandela. They were young and old, rich and poor, Muslim and Christian, straight and gay, educated and uneducated. Above all they were brothers, most of whom had met for the first time that day, but whose sense of family, camaraderie, and love was akin to that of long-lost friends united after years of separation.

This book, appropriately titled *Atonement: The Million Man March,* distills the emotions, insights, and visions of one million African Americans into the thoughtful reflections of fifty men.

These are the stories of fathers and sons, teachers and students, laborers and scholars, all expressing their hope and their joy in the oneness of this uncommon, if not once in a lifetime, experience.

Their words will challenge, uplift, and encourage us all to strive for those lofty principles that were at the very heart of this history-making event.

Excerpts: From a
Black Woman to a Black Man

MAYA ANGELOU

Voices of old, spirit sound
Speak to us in words profound
Across the years and centuries
Across the oceans and rolling seas

"Draw near to each other
Value your race
You were paid for dearly
In another place."

"The hell you have lived through
And live through still
Has sharpened your senses
And toughened your will."

The night has been long
The wounds have been deep
The pit has been dark
The walls have been steep.

I look through your anguish
Down into your soul
And know that together
We can be made whole.

The Million Man March Pledge

I pledge that from this day forward, I will strive to love my brother as I love myself.

I, from this day forward, will strive to improve myself spiritually, morally, mentally, socially, politically, and economically for the benefit of myself, my family, and my people.

I pledge that I will strive to build businesses, build houses, build hospitals, build factories, and enter into international trade for the good of myself, my family, and my people.

I pledge that from this day forward, I will never raise my hand with a knife or a gun to beat, cut, or shoot any member of my family or any human being except in self-defense.

I pledge from this day forward, I will never abuse my wife by striking her, disrespecting her, for she is the mother of my children and the producer of my future.

I pledge that from this day forward, I will never engage in the abuse of children, little boys, or little girls for sexual gratification. I will let them grow in peace to be strong men and women for the future of our people.

I will never again use the B-word to describe any female—but particularly, my own Black sister.

I pledge from this day forward that I will not poison my body with drugs or that which is destructive to my health and my well-being.

I pledge from this day forward, I will support Black newspapers, Black radio, Black television. I will support Black artists who clean up their act to show respect for their people and respect for the heirs of the human family.

I will do all of this, so help me God.

REFLECTIONS

A View from a Hill

RONALD S. BONNER SR.

It was a God-ordained day with a piercing blue sky. From the first ray of sunlight that broke through the predawn black velvet curtain to the moment that we gathered on the train to ride into D.C., to the fullness of coming onto the dawnlit Mall, where already one hundred thousand or more men had begun to fellowship. We knew that this was going to be a special day.

By eight in the morning, the speakers had started to express their joy of being there. In their voices was heard the strain of holding back the torrents of pride that was swelling within them as they spoke to this assemblage of Black men—African American men, who came from every walk of life, who walked or moved to this site, this Mecca, on this day. I saw African American men carrying oxygen tanks and men carrying babies to this place to listen, to stand, and to vow to make this a better world for our children, our families, our communities, and the world.

We listened to the voices of those who had been in the struggle for thirty years or more. There was the sweet voice of resistance as Rosa Parks spoke; there was the melodic voice of perseverance as Maya Angelou spoke. There was the promising voice of Allendye Baptiste Jr. as he called on us to be protectors of our race.

We stood tall as Cedars and proud as lions that day. African American men stood shoulder to shoulder, 150 wide and 10,000 deep. We stood as deep as the ocean that claimed the lives of nearly forty million Africans who died during the Middle Passage. We stood men of every hue and demeanor. Some had hair as white as the top of Mount Kilimanjaro; others, being carried by their fathers, wore diapers and had just a wisp of hair. We stood on that Mall, we stood on the side streets, we stood by the Washington Monument, and we stood down by the White House.

As we listened and as we stood, we were being bathed in the light of God. And in this light we were breaking the image of darkness that had shrouded us for far too long. Here were over a million Black men gathered in a peaceful demonstration in front of God, the government, and the world, saying by our presence that we are not a vile and virulent people, but that we are God-loving and God-fearing, and that as a people we can unite and be moral agents for social change. So we vowed to make a difference in the world. We vowed to be better men, fathers, husbands, uncles, and friends to all who need us. We vowed to end the various forms of violence that we engage in as a result of over four hundred years of oppression against our own. We vowed to atone for our sins and to be responsible for the lives that we affect. And we vowed to love.

This day was more than a march on Washington by a million Black men. It was a day of Black on Black love being born. You ask what else I saw? I saw a new heaven and a new earth; for the former had passed away, and there were no more divisions and God dwelled within.

The March before the March

SHAWN M. BARNEY

Student activism has long been a part of the college experience. The causes that one chooses to champion often define who one is and what one will become in the future. As first-year college students embark on their four-year college experience with eagerness as impressionable youth, they are largely aware of the importance of improving the conditions of Blacks in America. Thus, my learning experience at Howard University has transcended the classroom. It has made me realize that in many cases, the whole is more important than the parts, and that active participation is often preferable to watching as a passive observer.

At Howard we staged our own predawn "March before the March" on October sixteenth. Before marching to the capitol, students from around the country convened on our campus for a rally. To lead a group of my male peers in support of such a profound cause was a very humbling experience. Our exercise in unity for a common cause was a microcosm of the reasoning that underscored why African Americans had to march on the Capitol Mall.

When European Americans heard about the March, they felt threatened and became nervous. They should not have. The idea of a student march and the larger Million Man March was devised because of a need for cultural, intellectual, and social emphasis on issues that correlate exclusively with the identity of people of African decent.

Our student effort, like the larger effort, recognized that European Americans never can understand what African Americans have been through. They must respect our experiences and learn to deal with the questions of how to help. Howard and other historically Black colleges and universities teach students to confront these questions. Our student march was a recognition of the need for us to take our knowledge and teach it to the wider community.

I had an opportunity to speak at the Million Man March. In fact, I was a confirmed speaker who took the liberty of alerting family, friends, and even foes of the distinct opportunity before me. In short, October sixteenth was to be a day of individual triumph for me. However, the sixteenth resulted in a day of personal disappointment.

Because of extremely tight security, changes in the speakers' schedule, and miscommunication, I remained less than ten feet away from the podium. I watched my dream of speaking fade with each speaker. Yet I am glad. My failure to speak provided a better backdrop for me to understand the purpose of the March.

In order to understand why the Million Man March was necessary, one would have to understand the various reasons given by the millions of people who supported it. More importantly, however, one must understand that the Million Man March was not about individual agendas, accolades, or opportunities. To accept any of these reasons would devalue its historical relevance.

This reminds me of the narrow definition that some people apply to the meaning of africentricity. Some people believe that africentricity is exclusionary and that it belittles the heritage of other people. To the contrary, the March was supported by people all over the world and gave witness to the accomplishments of responsible Black men.

The March symbolized an effort to make amends for many of the ills that plague the African American community. Similarly, it also represented an effort to reconcile transgressions within oneself. The Million Man March did not intend to blame Whites or any other group for what their ancestors did to hinder the progress of African Americans. However, because many of the obstacles that African Americans face have been institutionalized over the passage of time, European Americans must be held accountable for eliminating them.

The March clearly showed the commitment that African American men need to make to their communities and families. Thus, the March was patriotic because of its direct correlation with improving America as a whole.

To understand the March one must understand the struggle of people of African descent. Ours is a struggle that has always been about independence in America and not separation from it. We are undoubtedly American by birth. The question is whether we will remain American by privilege or whether we will prevail as Americans by right.

Student activism has taught me a lot. I have chosen to champion this struggle in the days, months, and years beyond the Million Man March.

What Happens When No One Comes?

RICHARD M. BUNDY JR.

I attended the Million Man March held in Washington, D.C., on October 16, 1995. As a leader of a large, progressive church in Chicago, I felt it my responsibility to support the unifying agenda of the March. I am so very happy that I did, because it was such a positive event. I left there feeling refreshed and energized—with new hope and vision.

On the return trip, we had ample time for reflection. Someone raised the question of what each of us planned to do once we got home. Discussion centered around our responsibilities to the community and what each of us hoped to accomplish in our various churches.

I chose to become involved in prison ministry since so many African American men are incarcerated. I had already started to establish the basis for prison ministry before I left to attend the March. When I returned home, my passion and calling for this ministry were clear.

For a long time I noticed that prison ministry was one of the areas in which the African American church should bow its head in shame. The church has deserted these brothers and sisters. Many African American churches fail to acknowledge our present condition as it relates to the incarcerated. One reason the vast majority of African American churches fail to act is because of the image of "us and them." This image continues to operate on a subliminal plane. The church plays an ambiguous role in the formation of self-nurturing but also providing a religious justification for the false (masked) self. The mask creates a false consciousness of "us and them," the free and the incarcerated.

The Million Man March broke down this image and enabled me to see and feel that I had to become deeply involved. It helped me to take off my own mask and become more involved in the community.

When I reflect on the life of Jesus throughout the Gospels, he always seemed to show up at the address of those who were alienated or ostracized. In fact, Jesus seemed to gravitate to poor and disenfranchised people. He interacted with the throwaways of society. He walked with those with whom society said you shouldn't walk. Through the life of Jesus, the church has been given the mandate to heal the sick, encourage those who have lost hope, and touch those persons no one wants to touch.

The issue of prison ministry in the context of the March has had a powerful impact on me. Professionally, I have always been assigned to middle-class churches which have viewed, to some degree, the incarcerated as invisible.

In my personal life, I have always felt a connection to those who are incarcerated. In the late 1940s, my uncle, Charles Lyons, received a life sentence for murder. I know him only through the limited stories my family shared about him. There was a secrecy in the way they spoke about him. Conversations were always in hushed tones and with regretful words that bespoke shame and guilt—guilt because most of the family stopped visiting him except for my mother and maternal grandmother.

In my youthful, simplistic mind, I must have categorized him as an evil man. During my teenage years, my mother would return home after visiting her brother with gifts he had made. Sometimes they were arts and crafts that had been constructed with great skill. On one occasion, he sent me a model ship. It was beautifully made. You could tell that it took a lot of time to construct such a masterpiece. Although I was impressed with the gift, I don't remember writing my uncle to say "Thank you." As an adult, I now can imagine the pain of rejection that my uncle must have felt. He had reached out to me, his nephew, and I did nothing to affirm his existence.

It has been thirty years since his death. Today, I understand so much more about the complexity of life than that simplistic boy who so easily formed opinions about evil and good many years ago. Attending the Million Man March shed a rich light on my feelings about being "connected" to something bigger than myself.

This awakening involved many late-night, long-distance phone calls to family and friends to piece together our collective memories. I wanted to know the exact date my uncle died, where he was laid to rest, and whether or not any of our relatives were present at his funeral. This experience has provided rich new insights into my family. Much healing has taken place in this endeavor. Mostly, it has reconnected us on a deeper level by shining the light of forgiveness into the closet of family secrecy.

The impact on my life after the Million Man March has prompted me to write a letter to my uncle and a response that he might have written:

Dear Uncle Charles,

I know this letter is thirty years overdue and you are very surprised to hear from me after all this time. Perhaps you thought we might be separated for all eternity, but it has taken this long for me to come to myself.

You and I never saw each other, but I heard stories about you. I feel that I know you in a way that is deeper than any photograph and beyond any physical images.

I remember when you sent me a model ship, and Lainey, a dresser. It must have really hurt you never to receive a response from us. I regret that we never had a chance to know each other as uncle and nephew.

Nevertheless, I want you to understand something. When my mother spoke about you, I could see in her eyes the real pride she had in you. Her glances hinted to us that you possessed very good qualities. I know that doesn't matter to you now, but my memory of you will live on in my work. The question that will always be paramount in my mind is "What happens when no one comes?" I will remember you and what I failed to do.

When family and friends come to me confused and in pain, asking if they should forget about their loved ones in prison, asking if they should go on with their lives, I will remember you. I will tell them to gather together and hold hands. This will be a torch to help them find their way.

Your life was not in vain. Even though brothers and sisters continue to cry from the prisons of this country for personhood,

I know that you had to develop strong family relationships in prison because we denied that to you. Those persons probably seemed more like family than we did.

I want you to know that I, your blood relative, through the unction of the Holy Spirit, will work to set the captives free. Finally, nothing can separate us from the love of God — not prison, nor time, nor the world to come. One day we will see God face to face. Then we will know.

Love is stronger than death,

 Richard

Following is the response that I envision from my uncle:

Dear Richard,

When I read your letter, I felt as though a spring that had dried up long ago had begun to produce the first drops of water. Your words are like arrows of light that have traveled through eternity to rest in my heart.

For a long time I expected no response from my family, because I was mentally wiped out by the misery that daily confronted me. The pain of never hearing a familiar voice or seeing a familiar face stretched out to months and years. I held faded photographs that never spoke to me, except in the deep recesses of my mind.

No one knew of my talents and gifts and wonderful sense of humor. Neither did they know of my capacity to be a friend to the friendless. For years I hurt deep inside and I thought there was no way to fix the hurt. I felt betrayed and alone. My dreams were turned to dust because nobody came.

Never will I forget the feeling of loneliness and isolation when no one visited during holidays. Christmas and Easter became mere dates on the calendar that marked the stripping away of who I was. Gradually this separation from my family caused a deep hole in my soul. That hole became filled with demons that constantly attempted to destroy my faith.

I had no one to cry for me, and my life had become a footnote on the margin of the world's history. It was as if I never existed except for a birth and death certificate. Many times I felt as if my own mother had abandoned me and there was no one to hold me.

I kept trying to grasp things around me, attempting to find meaning for my life, hoping that whatever I grasped could grasp me too. But I discovered that no experience is more powerful than a glance, the interplay of eyes, looking at someone who is looking at you, or the experience of being seen.

All of this happened to me, yet I never forgot you or others. The need to be seen, to be recognized, gives meaning to everybody's life, even if you are locked away in some prison or a place where nobody wants to be. Everything else—life, food, shelter and being warm—mean little unless you have meaning.

My suffering and my stories remain untold to human ears, but God has allowed the Holy Spirit to travel through the gulf that separates us, because your heart is right and you bring an incredible gift after all these years. I am glad that model ship brought you to a place in the mind of God where those who are imprisoned are not forgotten.

Press on,

Charles Lyons

Enough to Make a Difference

THOMAS E. WORTHAM III

As my son and I arrived at Midway Airport on the morning of October 16, 1995, I was in a state of wonderment. I did not know what to expect. Rev. Farrakhan had called for a million men to come to Washington, D.C., for Atonement. I knew that never in history had a million Black men come together for anything. And truthfully, I did not expect a million men to show up. But I did feel that even if two hundred thousand showed up, it would be worth being there.

The number of Black men that were waiting to depart on flights to Washington should have been a hint to me of what was to come. As I walked through the airport, I saw more Black men than I had ever seen in my life. This raised my curiosity even more. When my son and I arrived at our gate, we met the other forty or fifty men from Trinity United Church of Christ who were also going to the March on our flight. We all greeted one another with handshakes and hugs, glad to come together for such an event. We all prayed together before boarding the plane.

After landing in Washington, I was in awe at the number of Black men I saw at the airport. It was at this time that I began to suspect that I was in for more than I could ever imagine in my wildest dreams. As we boarded buses to take us to the train station, I saw more men heading to the March.

When we arrived at the train station, all I could see were lines of Black men with signs indicating where they were from and what organization they belonged to. As we boarded the train en route to the Mall, it was loaded with men and women heading to the same place.

I had never experienced such a warm feeling between myself and total strangers as I did on the bus and train. We all were greeting and talking to one another as if we were old friends. This was a wonderful feeling. I began thinking that something wonderful was about to happen.

When we finally arrived at the Mall, I was shocked. All I could see was a sea of Black men and women. Never before in my life had I seen so many Black people together at one time. It was the most beautiful sight I had ever seen. I was in total awe at the number of people. I had no idea how many people were there, but it was more than I had expected to see.

At this time I felt a sigh of relief. It was as if a burden had been taken off my back. I guess I was worried that the turnout would not be significant enough to be meaningful. But at this time, I knew it was enough to make a difference.

As I walked around the Mall, I felt a spiritual calmness among the people. Never before had I experienced such a large number of people coming together with such a feeling of peace and together-ness. I knew God had to have a hand in this. There were people from all walks of life, from all over the country greeting one an-other in the spirit of love.

What now? It is my belief that the most important thing African American people can do in their daily lives is to adopt the spirit of oneness, caring, politeness, and courtesy and the concept of "each one, teach one." If we all add the aforementioned values to our daily lives, we can overcome all of the problems with which our communities are presently plagued.

If the spirit and attitude that were present at the March spread through the African American community, we would see an imme-diate decrease in the crime and violence that are now prevalent. Accompanying the decrease in violence would be a new pride in our neighborhoods—cleaner streets, no graffiti.

The African American community would also experience a re-surgence in Black businesses. African Americans would take pride in spending their money in Black-owned businesses. A resurgence in Black businesses would lead to an increase in Black employment, resulting in less poverty and healthier communities. This would also lead to a stronger economic base for the Black community, which would allow the community to be in charge of its own des-tiny and not to be dependent on people outside of the community for its existence.

In order for the African American community to ever have parity with other, non-Black communities, we must have control over our economy and have a larger say in the politics that govern our daily lives. We can only do this by coming together as a community.

Gays and the Million Man March

KEITH BOYKIN

"Black by Birth/Gay by God/Proud by Choice." Those were the words my trembling hands scribbled on the posterboard in the brisk morning air at a Black gay rally a few hours before the Million Man March.

Hundreds of Black gay men and a handful of lesbians joined together in a historic openly gay contingent in the Million Man March, proudly representing the tens of thousands of Black gay men who were there but could not be a part of our group. Our pre-March rally drew prominent speakers from around the country, including noted law school professor and civil rights activist Derrick Bell, who is heterosexual, and the Black, openly gay mayor of Cambridge, Massachusetts, Kenneth Reeves.

Uncertain of what lay ahead, we left our rally and quietly began the thirty-minute procession to the March assembly on the Capitol Mall. A few passersby hurriedly moved out of the way, two people driving their cars along the adjoining streets honked their horns in support, and a number of pedestrians stopped and stared.

Sensing no negative reaction, our group grew increasingly ambitious and empowered. We began to chant: "We're Black! We're gay! We wouldn't have it any other way!" Still, no one in the crowd of people we approached reacted critically.

The lesson in this experience is that when we believe in ourselves, other people believe in us, too. When we believe in ourselves enough to come out of the closet and be open about who we are as Black gay men and lesbians, our community not only accepts us, it respects us more. October sixteenth was the first time that many March participants had ever seen Black homosexuals openly, visibly and unabashedly acknowledging themselves as a part of the Black community. Given the opportunity to succumb to peer-pressure prejudice, they took the high road and greeted our participation. They know that the battle for Black liberation requires many soldiers, and in this army, at least, gays are welcome in the military.

What happened on the Mall that day was the beginning of a revolution in our thinking as Black people and as Black gay people. Black men loving Black men is a revolutionary act. In a culture whose popular music and film glorify Blacks' violence toward other Blacks, the simple act of loving our brothers as brothers becomes an act of rebellion against fratricide.

Who is better suited to help Black men learn the value of loving one another as brothers than Black gay men, who have been loving one another as brothers for years? Who is better suited to demonstrate to Black men how to care for and show affection for one another than Black gay men, who have been caring for and showing affection toward one another when no one else would? And who is better suited to lead the long-overdue revolution against patriarchy and violence against women than Black gay men? Indeed, as Black Panther leader Huey Newton presciently observed in 1970, "a homosexual could be the most revolutionary" of the revolutionaries.

Despite the welcome extended by March participants, the organizers and speakers missed two crucial opportunities: First, to include an openly gay speaker and, second, to teach Black men how to save their lives in this era of AIDS; prevention was never discussed. Unfortunately, the disease will continue to take a toll on our community so long as Black people and our so-called leaders remain too afraid to address publicly issues of sex, sexuality, and sexual orientation.

Nevertheless, I hope the presence of our openly gay contingent will help to begin the much needed dialogue on Black sexuality and teach the organizers what the vast majority of rank-and-file marchers already know: Black gay men and lesbians are not a threat to Black unity, they are a key to it.

A Religious Experience

JEREMIAH A. WRIGHT JR.

The National Day of Atonement was a "once in a lifetime" experience for my son and for me. Prior to the March, I had been involved in several discussions, debates, and arguments with other Christian ministers about whether or not those of us who follow Christ should go to Washington, D.C. Some conservative and fundamentalist African American preachers felt that no Christian should support the March, simply because the man who issued the call for a million Black men to gather in Washington was a Muslim.

Worse than being an orthodox Muslim, the convener of the March was a Black Muslim, the head of Elijah Muhammad's Nation of Islam. Even worse than that, the convener, Minister Louis Farrakhan, is considered anti-Semitic, a race baiter, a sexist, a misogynist, and a demagogue. "Can anything good come out of Nazareth?" "Or a mosque on the south side of Chicago?" "Or Farrakhan's mind or his mouth?"

Rev. Benjamin Chavis, a United Church of Christ minister, did the actual organizing of the March; however, this was not to be taken into consideration at all. Just the mention of Rev. Chavis's name muddied the waters even further. After all, he had just been "fired" from the NAACP for his sexist, misogynist behavior.

There were progressive and liberal African American clergy who were also against the March. The reason conservatives gave was that they had marched with Dr. Martin Luther King Jr. They felt Minister Farrakhan had disrespected, and in fact publicly disparaged, Black preachers for over a quarter of a century! These preachers refused to be used by him. They, therefore, openly, vociferously, and vigorously opposed the March and Minister Farrakhan. It was with these clergy members—male and female—that I argued, debated, talked, and prayed concerning October 16, 1995.

Moreover, there were several women, clergy and lay, who where opposed to the March because of the Muslim position on women and the sexist comments of its convener. They could not understand how any sensitive or caring United Church of Christ clergy member could possibly support any movement backed by or called by a man like Louis Farrakhan. And they told me so in no uncertain terms, both verbally and in writing!

Prior to the March, I had been engaged in several different discussions, debates, dialogues, and arguments with other Christians and non-Christians. We discussed whether or not it made sense for Christians to follow the lead of one who seemed diametrically opposed to that same Christ. Nevertheless, the actual day was a once in a lifetime experience for me and for my son—notwithstanding the prelude and preliminaries!

I was actually one of the speakers on the program; or I should say, I was scheduled to be a speaker on the program. I was scheduled to speak between Maya Angelou and Allendye Baptiste, who attends my son's school, somewhere between 11:30 and 11:45 A.M. The program coordinators got off the phone with me at 3:00 A.M. on Monday, verifying our flight number and arrival time. They assured me that a car would be there to pick us up. But when we arrived in Washington, D.C., there was no car.

My son Nathan and I waited for fifteen minutes. Since it was almost 10:20 A.M., we walked over to the Metro along with hundreds of other men and entered into an experience that can only be described as a "religious experience."

We arrived on the Mall and saw over a million men and women. My son's fourteen-year-old expression made the day and the trip worthwhile. Nathan said, "Wow!" His mouth stayed open, and his eyes were as wide as saucers. Even though the car never arrived, even though I could not get near the platform, and even though I would not speak at such a historic moment in American history, it did not matter anymore.

The only thing that mattered was that a fourteen-year-old African American boy, who has been labeled an "endangered species" by sensitive sociologists, had gotten to witness a million Black men standing together. They stood to affirm their women, their culture, and to ask God for grace to be the husbands, fathers, lovers, sons, and warriors that God needs in order for all our people to be free.

The Nation of Islam only numbers around 40,000 persons nationwide; so the 960,000-plus "others" on October sixteenth were overwhelmingly Christians. On our plane, for instance, 115 out of 120 passengers going to the March were Christians. On the flight that left an hour before our flight, there were 80 men and women from Trinity United Church of Christ. Trinity had 516 persons at the March; 200 flew on several different carriers, and the others rode buses, trains, and cars. They came on behalf of all African Americans who are determined to be free.

The spirit of that day was infectious, and the local organizing committees around the country all worked feverishly to carry out various "pieces" of the dream that each of them had decided to own.

In Chicago, both the local organizing committee and the local church/mosque/civic committees, born out of the March, are working to do what they can in their chosen areas.

At Trinity United Church of Christ, our "Million for the Master" committee is conducting weekly voter registration drives at every gathering of the congregation. On the day of the March, 516 participants pledged to register 8 voters each. The church committee has set a goal to register 4,100 voters before the November elections.

The Men's Bible class has changed its weekly closing from a pledge written by Dr. Jawanza Kunjufu, a Trinity member and March speaker, to the pledge that was taken by the participants at the March. Each week the men are reminded of their promises to God to respect our women, to respect ourselves, to engage in economic development, and to be active participants in the household of faith.

As a local church pastor, I have seen a new spirit break out in the congregation because of the March. I have seen persons who never worked on anything in their church now working to register voters, to mentor young men and women, to learn the Bible, and to become intentional about their spirituality. I have seen new members join the church as a result of the March, and I have seen the spirit of God moving in our community in ways I had never seen before.

In many ways it feels like "mine eyes have seen the glory of the coming of the Lord!" It is my prayer that the entire church—Black, White, Hispanic, American Indian, and Asian—will be captured by the Spirit and work on God's agenda to "set the captives free!"

I Want to Be in That Number

NATHAN WARREN REED

The National Day of Atonement and Reconciliation, which is also known as the day of the Million Man March, was a day for healing. It was a day that African American men (and a few women) came together from all over America to take a stand and to make positive personal changes.

There were men with different backgrounds sharing laughs and love. There were men with different religious beliefs and men who represented a wide variety of occupations. Together they all locked step and locked arms on the Mall in Washington, D.C.

I saw men from different fraternities. There were men who attended with different problems and reasons, but they came to unite as one. There were strong African American men who stood together publicly and made amends. They promised to address the problems in their communities and the problems in their homes. There were men from all over the world sharing stories.

People, young and old, shared their stories, their problems, and their determination to resolve the issues that we face as an African American people. The Million Man March was the most memorable experience I have ever had!

In the beginning, I did not think I was going to be able to get to the March. I had seen many newscasts about the National Day of Atonement. As October sixteenth drew closer, I imagined what the sight of a million men would be like. I wondered how I would react or how I would feel if I were there.

I wanted to be in that number. I wanted to be at the Million Man March. Students at school talked about it. Nobody said anything about it in my household. I did not think I would get there. I knew that the Million Man March was going to be a historic event. But for weeks, I thought the March would be a historic event that I would miss.

Many of my friends from school were going, and others who could not go were staying home from school to support the National Day of Atonement. We were being asked to stay home by the convener of the March to discuss our history, to make plans to do positive things in our churches and in our communities. The March was the main item of discussion by the African American students around school. We talked about atonement activities. We talked about where worship services would be held. We talked about what our teachers might think about the March, because none of them said anything about it in class.

It seemed as though only the African American teachers and school administrators were supporting the March. Nevertheless, all of my classmates were determined that they were going to take part in this historical moment. I was going to stay home like my classmates to show my support. I had heard my mother mention that my baby sister would be home, so I knew I had my parents' support to stay home. Additionally, we were also having a National Day of Atonement worship service at our church.

On October fourteenth, my father, Rev. Jeremiah A. Wright Jr., the pastor of Trinity United Church of Christ in Chicago, told me that I was going to the March with him. I was speechless! I was excited! I was almost beside myself!

On October fifteenth, I went to bed anxious for morning to come. The next day, we left at 4:00 A.M. to catch a 6:30 flight to Washington, D.C. I got dressed faster than ever that morning. I couldn't wait to be in that number. I couldn't wait to be a part of history!

As my father and I drove to the airport, we listened to the disc jockeys who were also ecstatic as they described the turnout for the March. The Black stations in Chicago were broadcasting live from the March, and the broadcasters—male and female—were excited as they reported how many people were on the Mall as early as midnight and one o'clock that morning!

They told us that men were singing and praying. These people were making preparations for history to take place. I couldn't wait to get in that number! We arrived at O'Hare Airport to see hundreds of serious men who wanted to unite for atonement. It was awesome!

I had never seen so many serious men ready for action and ready for change. I saw over a hundred men from my church, and it felt like my heart would beat right out of my chest!

When we got to Washington, we were not picked up by the car that the coordinators had promised my father, so we caught the Metro along with thousands of other African American men. We exited the Metro station and walked to the Mall. There are no words to describe what my eyes saw!

The sight of African American men—a million strong—inspired me to become the best that I can in everything! I was thrilled to listen to Maya Angelou tell of the past and brilliance of African men. I was blessed to hear her speaking about the intelligence, the power, and the specialties that only Black men have. Maya Angelou even spoke about my generation. She ended her powerful speech by telling men to look up because "Still We Will Rise!" I thought she was talking directly to me!

Now, many months later, I have thought about what we as Black men can do. African American men need to give their lives to Christ. If men would stop being so "macho" and get some morals, we would be a different people. I think men need to stop "tripping." Many of the songs that my peers listen to have language that disrespects our Black women. This disrespect is a part of what I mean by "tripping." We need to stop.

We as Black people—men and women—need to wake up. The March was our wake-up call. We need to start praying and put down the pistols!

We need God, and we need guidance. Today men need to participate in church activities and to help one another to succeed. These are the things that I am determined to do now, as well as for the rest of my life. The Million Man March was an event that changed my life, and with God as the head of my life and Christ as the Lord of my life, I have no doubt that I will succeed!

I believe that we need to stop pointing the finger at one another and at other things, and just go on and make a change. The change needs to start with us! African Americans need to be more responsible. Men should take care of their families and stop making babies that they do not support.

Every night, kids kill kids because they have no supervision. Men should start caring instead of killing! We need to realize that what we are doing is hurting and not helping!

Churches should take the lead to address these problems. My church and others have programs for men to join. It is my prayer that more African American churches will take the lead—captured by the spirit of the March—to address these problems and to turn this situation around.

No Ordinary Day

NEIL JAMES BULLOCK

Standing on the platform of the Amtrak/commuter rail station in Baltimore, I had no idea what the day would bring for me. I was full of anticipation, but what I did not anticipate was an Amtrak train speeding by at what seemed a million miles per hour. The train came out of nowhere without a sound, taking many other African American men on the platform and myself by surprise. After the train passed, I was a bit on edge but not as much as a young, well-dressed, White man nervously reading his paper. He was trying to be inconspicuous among the growing crowd of Black men. Although he was trying to go about his normal day, it was becoming obvious to all of us that this was not going to be an ordinary day.

Later I and four other brothers from Chicago who were traveling with me arrived at Union Station. We had planned to meet the son of one of the brothers and his friends in the main terminal of the station. When we got to the main terminal it was as though war had been declared, and African American men were gathering there waiting to receive orders. People were moving around shoulder to shoulder. They all seemed to be wondering where to go and what to do next. Very soon it became apparent to us that we were not going to find my friend's son. We made plans in case we got separated from one another and moved on.

I waited outside a camera shop in the terminal while my friends made last-minute purchases. Like everyone else, I was looking for familiar faces among the crowd when a voice caught my attention. There was a brother standing next to me dressed in traditional African clothes, wearing a turban with a Star of David on it. Another brother passing by stopped and asked him who he was and where was he from. I thought this was very bold of this man, but it was probably his character: He had a commanding presence and an out-going personality. He said that he was an Orthodox Jew from Phila-delphia and that whenever he saw someone "wearing his stuff," meaning the Star of David, he wanted to know who they were. The African American man wearing the Star of David said he was also a Jew. They talked for a while, exchanging addresses, and parted saying that they would hook up again in Philadelphia.

As a Black Lutheran, that moment confirmed for me that this March was not about any particular religious conviction. This March was about spiritual oneness for us as a people. Not since the civil rights movement had I witnessed such a sense of unity in the Afri-can American community. Christians, Jews, Muslims, and others were all in Washington together for one reason. We were there to prove that African American men are not powerless in this country and that we are able to mobilize our collective awareness.

As we left the station, we followed streams of men walking in the same direction. When we arrived at the Mall in front of the Capitol, I was stunned to see masses of Black men. As far as I could see, there was a sea of Black men. I had never seen so many people in one place at one time, and I imagined I never would see such a sight again. There we were: all shapes, sizes, colors, and ages; fa-thers with sons, uncles, and brothers. It was truly a family affair.

I believe that most of the men at the March were either like me, with friends, or with family members. Fathers, sons, brothers, and uncles were all in Washington for one reason—atonement. The ques-tion was "atonement for what?" There may be many things that one could say African American men need to atone for, not the least of which is the sin of disrespect. We have been disrespectful to our women, families, communities, and most of all to ourselves.

Next to disrespect is the sin of believing what "White society" has said about us. We have been told that we are not taking respon-sibility for the care of our families; that we are violent; and that we deserve nothing better than to be locked away from society. Far too many of us have believed these negative reports and have acted accordingly. Our young men are neither valued nor nurtured. As a result of a lack of investment in the education and development of our young people by our own community, we have reared a whole generation of people who do not have a sense of support from the African American community as a family. The support I knew growing up in Philadelphia was so strong that no matter how much wrong there was in the world, my home and community were a safe place.

As African American men, we needed a day of atonement—a time when we could say to ourselves that the problems we face as a people can only be solved by ourselves. We needed to atone collectively as well as individually for allowing drugs, violence, and other destructive forces to rule our communities. We needed a voice from within the community to say to us that something is wrong in the community. Minister Farrakhan was that voice.

For whatever reason, a million-plus Black men came to hear the voice of Minister Farrakhan and others. Regardless of the controversy about Farrakhan, many thousands of non-Muslim brothers united for a divine purpose. The spirituality of that time and place was in the unity of the African American man. On that day, African American men showed the world that we are respectful, orderly, disciplined, and taking charge of our own destiny. This gives me hope for the future. The message was clear. We need to begin to do for ourselves.

So, the question now is "What must we do?" If all the men attending the March were asked what needs to be done to bring about atonement for our sins, there would probably be a million different answers.

I believe we need to atone for economic dependency. For too long, we have waited for the government to be the instrument of our salvation. When we see the decay of our communities and the lack of opportunities for our children, it is also the result of our own shortcomings. We need to invest in our own future. Billions of dollars go through our community, yet we do not pull our resources together to create industry. I feel that each and every one of us has a responsibility, wherever he or she is, to give some of his or her personal resources back to the community.

If we would commit to spending even a portion of our personal resources at Black-owned businesses, Wall Street would take notice. When I see the trash from packaging material, glass, and aluminum that litters the streets of our neighborhoods, I am pained to realize that others have profited from us and all we have is the refuse. Nothing is manufactured, yet we provide a market for goods to be sold. If we were a separate nation, we would recognize the imbalance of trade and begin to take steps to correct that imbalance.

I have resolved to spend *no less* than one-tenth of all my income in the African American community. By taking economic action, we can begin to build a base to create our own wealth. When the call went out at the March to collect an offering to start an economic development fund, I felt that this was a way in which I could personally do something to help my people as a whole. When I saw thousands of African American men holding up their money, there was a sense of power in the air. I realized that we can do anything we set our minds to as a people. I was proud of my brothers, and I believe that the spirit of collective cooperation will continue.

I am a part of a mentoring program for young Black males. African American men must reach out and save our children. African American men need to invest themselves in the children and young men and women in our communities. As a Christian, I believe that God is on our side and will give us what we need to make a difference. God has already empowered us to make a difference. We must use the power we have—*love*. When we love God and one another, things will change.

The Choice

ALEX PICKENS JR.

As I attempted to gather some thoughts about the Million Man March, the realization struck that whether you were for or against the March, everyone must choose sides. It is difficult to explain why I supported the March. It is perhaps more difficult to understand why the March was not supported by all; particularly disappointing was the fact that our National Baptist leaders did not officially support the March. These leaders may be out of touch with who God is and unable to see a true view of the solution to our present societal problems, especially as they relate to Black men in urban areas. The maladies are now critical.

Early on, I had prepared to attend the March. As the date approached, my determination increased. I had asked my eighteen-year-old high school son if he wanted to attend. He was very enthusiastic. I also have a twenty-one-year-old son who attends Howard University in Washington, D.C. I asked him about attending the March. He indicated that his minister "was cool" to the idea of the March and was particularly cool to Farrakhan. Somewhere during this time, it became clear that the problems affecting our people cannot be managed by others. We must now, more than ever, stop being our own worst enemies. We must rid ourselves of this self-defeating sense of apathy.

The ride to Washington, D.C., was very smooth. There was an incredible amount of traffic on the turnpike through Ohio and Pennsylvania. We stayed at my nephew's house. We were made welcome as he had made my son welcome. My nephew is a young man just under thirty years old who allowed my son to share a grand old mansion in northwest Washington with him. My son and his cousin were enthusiastic and wanted to go to the March. Throughout the morning, several of their friends came by with news about the activities and preparations around the city.

There were two issues to note. First, the number of marchers was in question. This was another attempt to detract from the historical accomplishments of our people. It would certainly look good if the annals of history recorded that the largest assembly of marchers in our country had been African American men. Yet, the numbers were not important to me.

Second, the 1.2 million Black men who attended the March displayed the presence of calmness. This presence was everywhere. Even though it was difficult to hear the speeches in the area where we were standing, everyone enjoyed the ambiance more than the speeches. The power emanating from the group was overwhelming.

Finally, the Million Man March has compelled us to realize that there is a need for the relentless pursuit of education. We must provide security for our families. We need to set aside our fears and feel good about one another. We must allow ourselves to grow stronger from the success of the March. And we must return to our homes and start to bring an end to our self-destructive behavior.

A Lesson Well Received

ALEX PICKENS III

A sign of enlightenment in any individual is a reverence for the lessons learned through the study of history. Knowledge about one's extended family, ancestors, and even the struggles of parents gives a unique outlook on life—an outlook that is continually causing expansion of my consciousness. So when I was allowed to notice the folds and wrinkles in my father's face on the morning of October sixteenth, my understanding once again was expanded and I was brought closer to the truth.

In that autumn sun, the same love of Christ that was planted in Paul, Timothy, and Rudy Pickens manifested itself once again in the clear-eyed gaze of a city doctor from Birmingham, Alabama. His stare reminded me of the fact that the solutions sought at the March have always existed in human vessels. The solution is Christ.

The March was wonderful to many people for many reasons, but the revelations I received on that day have nothing to do with total strangers hugging one another or the pledge taken by 999,999 other men. The revelation I received on that day was the result of yet another seed of hope, planted in my name and soul decades ago, sprouting and bringing forth fruit. I am the personification of hopeful seeds planted in prayers offered years ago.

On reflection, I was not there for myself as much as I was there for my family and those that came before me. The greatest factor that influenced my decision to attend was not the message of the March or the organizer's charisma, but the tone and sincerity in my father's voice when he told me he was coming to visit. The joy in his voice overcame any tendency to stay away because of political or theological differences I might have had with the coordinators. I was there because my father was there.

Just as there is the hope of a proud lineage hidden in my bosom, there also abides in my father that same hope. The difference between him and me is that I have received a portion of his hope and confidence through my natural birth. Because I am his son, I become privy to the love within him and he becomes a part of the lineage of love. This privilege brings the opportunity to share in supporting the strength of youth, being next to my brother and under the adoring eye of the steward of the lineage. I hold the jewels of three hundred years within me. And so on that day in Washington, D.C., a story in our family history was told.

The March compiled the wealth passed through generations of instruction by example and reminded me that the answers to the questions that face my people are enhanced by committees, philosophy, discussion, and dialogue; they are not created by these things. The solutions sought on that day have been apparent to my lineage all along. The effectiveness of trusting in God, of committing to a steady, long-suffering method of Christ-centered childrearing, rather than seminar- and videotape-style parenting and faith, is evidenced in me. I am because of the Living Water that has flowed through my clan. I am because of the fire planted in my mother's instruction, which subdued the recklessness and disobedience of youth. None of these factors that aided my development came from the individual inspiration of my parents, but were placed in their minds by the God-fearing extension of my bloodline and their trust in Jesus.

Just as my mother's method of instruction was not her own, but an extension of God in her, so too was it the tone in my father's voice, which was not his own, that convinced me to accompany him to the March. I believe it was the incarnation of my clan in him, the handiwork of my God in him, beckoning me to the steps of the Capitol, so that yet another pearl of wisdom could be revealed to me. This lesson, revealed to me, I share with you.

Long Live the Spirit of the Million Man March

SETH W. PICKENS

I first heard about the Million Man March in the summer of 1995. As I took my usual drive down Davison, I saw some men selling copies of the *Final Call*. It was just another typical day, or so I thought. As I stopped at the red light, I could see the headline: "Why a Million Man March?" Good question, I thought, and proceeded to drive on in my usual way. For the next month or so, I heard very little about the March. One day, a local radio station personality came to my school to interview young Black men and women regarding their feelings on the March.

I really did not begin to think strongly about the March until my father asked me if I was interested in going. I had no reason *not* to participate since doing so would mean that I could be a part of history in the making. I could also visit my brother who lives in Washington and miss a day or two of school. The true spirit of the event evaded me until we actually arrived in Washington, D.C.

Upon arriving, my father and I stretched out on my brother's couch and watched the March on television until well into the afternoon. However, the more we watched, the more motivated we became to join the immense crowd. We hurried down to the March. As we approached the large throngs of men, there was a strong aroma in the air, and it wasn't the aroma of bean pies. It was unity! Strangers from rival fraternities embraced. Christians, Muslims, and atheists came together to celebrate their one true common bond. Women joined the March for different reasons. Some were feminists, blatantly defying the will of Minister Farrakhan. Most were just caught up in the spirit of the day and saw no problem in being there.

The smallest minority, Caucasians, had varying feelings also. Some were obviously uncomfortable, shuffling to get through the crowd to a meeting or to work. The vast majority of women and Caucasians, however, were there to support the spirit of the March. Despite what "we" think, showing up took a lot of courage on their part. We all tried to make them feel a part.

In short, the March itself was a very enlightening experience. The most important part is that all 999,999 of us must take what we learned and felt, and apply it to our lives.

From now on, October sixteenth is "our holy day." We should all remember the words of the chant led by Benjamin Chavis: "Long live the spirit of the Million Man March!"

A Family Reunion

MARTINI SHAW

The Million Man March was like a large family reunion of African American men. Yet it was more than a family reunion, because it included a very powerful, spiritual component. It was like refueling a fire. It was invigorating and enriching. People left Washington, D.C., with a great desire to work together. Like a revival, we came back excited, and we came back willing and wanting to do something for our community.

Sometimes the many problems that are occurring in the Black community are daunting, such as the state of the family or the state of the Black community as a whole. We have the tendency to say, "Oh God, there are so many things that need to be done, my little input will not be helpful." But if everyone took a small, minute interest and involvement in solving these issues, a difference could be made.

The Million Man March encouraged me to do that. It came at the right time, and I think it took the Holy Spirit to make it happen. I think men need to atone. There was a time for all of us to atone at the March, maybe some more than others, but still all together as one. We have not lived up to our responsibilities. None of us has been perfect.

I believe that something needs to occur now that the March has come and gone. There needs to be a follow-up, with a programmatic design for what we can do to improve the quality of life in our community. We must remember what inspired us to attend the March. This inspiration now must be translated into action. We should have annual or biennial marches. I think that the leaders of our community who attended the March should come together and design a strategy to make the vision of the March a reality.

I think there needs to be a stronger emphasis on mentoring. Finally, I think more churches and community groups should look at developing mentoring programs for our boys, who are now an endangered species.

Meeting the Challenge

ANDRÉ P. TRAMBLE

We, as African American men, undoubtedly have great challenges that confront us daily as we compete for our place in society. I have often reflected on these challenges and have often looked for the solutions to overcome those situations that are under my control. I remember once hearing it said that you have to stand for something, because if you don't, then you can fall for anything.

October 16, 1995, was the day that I decided to stand up! If you could have spoken to the more than one million Black men who attended the March in Washington, D.C., you would have heard a half-million reasons why they attended. More importantly, however, what you would have heard was that we, as African American men, needed to come together on this day!

Forget what you've heard in the media about the separatist views of Minister Farrakhan. I think the assembling of Black men was genius. I think it was a call that could not have been made by one person alone. This was a spiritual call in divine order.

It is a fact that people of color are segregated in the United States. Because of this, separatism should be placed in a larger perspective. In fact, this separatism could arguably be labeled as a major factor in the need for such a March. The Million Man March afforded me and other African American men an opportunity to act on one of the challenges that we are not known to face—that is, assembling in unity and in great numbers to confront our own problems. Of the many challenges we face, I often have felt that collectively we hold the key to unlocking the one treasure we devalued—that of self-respect! And self-pride!

Ironically, it only took one night of driving to see how important it is for African American men to come together and affirm our identity and to share a much stronger sense of Black pride and self-control.

The decision to attend the March was one of the easiest decisions I had ever made. I went with my good friend of more than

37

fifteen years, Eric. We connected spiritually on this decision. We had not discussed going to the March prior to his call to me. I was at work that day, feeling a deep sense of purpose about the March, when my phone rang. The first thing I said to Eric was, "Let's go to the March." The March was the reason why he had called. He was just as anxious as I was to go!

We drove to Washington, D.C., on the eve of the March not knowing what to expect. It did not take long for me to know that I would never forget this trip. Interestingly for me, the most defining moments of the March took place along the highway. You had to see it to appreciate it! The rest stops and toll booth plazas were electrifying. I had never seen so many Black men. We were all excited to see Black men in such large numbers! A deep sense of pride took over. It felt good to be received by my brothers with kind words, warm handshakes, and mutual respect for one another.

In order to appreciate the spirit that was omnipresent, you would have had to see the number of Black men who were everywhere. Men of all ages in bus after bus after bus, in car after car after car. I just sat in awe watching as cars and buses pulled into each of the the service areas where we made stops. I kept asking myself what was it that made these encounters so electrifying. What was so unexplainable about this scene? Then it dawned on me: It was the divine order that everybody magically adopted.

There was a real sense of calm and peacefulness. It was so pervasive that I finally realized just how many people were in pain. In the restroom, you could hear a Muslim brother saying words of inspiration to keep everyone focused. I'm not a Muslim, but you have to admit, if you have ever been in their company, you know those brothers are disciplined and orderly. I believe that their presence helped to define the unity and set the tone for the camaraderie that we would later need at the Mall.

I was very focused at this point. When we arrived at the hotel, I understood the historical significance associated with the March. I thought about the March's agenda. I became concerned that there would be one million African American men who would come as I did, full of pain and hope, only to leave without having our concerns and issues addressed.

I can't begin to explain the beautiful sight I saw when I arrived at the Mall that morning. If critics expected the March to be chaotic and disruptive, their expectations were unfounded. I thought, if we could come together in this orderly way and establish some commonsense principals of unity, how easily we could solve half of our self-imposed problems. It surprised me that I had this many Black brothers spread across the United States and that there were even more brothers back home, watching the March on television. I wondered if everyone would leave satisfied that something had been accomplished and that it had been more than just a rally.

I was pleased with the outcome, given the enormous task at hand. I therefore expected every brother to leave the Mall understanding what I believed:

- We, as African American men, should not have to be told that we should patronize our own businesses.

- We, as African American men, should not have to be told to respect ourselves, our women, and our families.

- We, as African American men, should not need to be told of our responsibilities as guardians of our children.

- Teenage gang leaders should know that if they continue the violence against other brothers, before long they will no longer have members left to recruit.

- We, as African American men, should know the importance of voting and marches.

- We, as African American men, would leave knowing the difference between four hundred thousand and one million.

I know the March held the attention of the U.S. Congress; however, I could just hear the condescending voices coming from the American people. We needed to take something home that we could immediately use in order to continue the unity and self-reliant attitude that were unmasked in Washington. The most effective means of destruction for our people lies in our inability to agree to disagree on a central ideal and come to a mutual compromise for harmony and progress. The simplest thing that African Americans could now do would be to regain our self-respect and respect for others.

The long-term goal that African American men should strive for is to educate our people. We need to develop the minds of our children. We should open alternative educational institutions for children from preschool through grade school. As a direct result, parents could select from a pool of schools that would provide a cultural background and a quality education. The only way we can be sure that our children are getting what they need is to administer it ourselves. I want to take this opportunity to thank Minister Farrakhan and Rev. Benjamin Chavis for their courage and vision in organizing a great beginning toward self-reliance for African American people. How about a Million Woman March followed by the development of a National Council on African American Educational School Systems?

A One-Time Experience

ERIC L. HILL

The Million Man March created that one-time experience in my life which I sometimes compare to the birth of my first daughter. To witness that beautiful event was a loving gift from God which I could never forget. Since the March, I sometimes reflect during the day on how a million Black men, African American men, unified for a cause that was seen by the entire world.

One evening prior to the March, I had been thinking that I would not *dream* of not attending the March. I knew that some people throughout the country were expressing strong opposition to it. I believed the opposition was based on negativity and fear. However, there were some individuals who were supportive of the March.

I felt that going to the March without a true friend or without a brother who was as concerned as I regarding the outlook and future of African American men would be a disservice to myself and our people. I discussed these concerns with my wife, who accepted that I would go to the March. Her affirmation allowed my strength and commitment to grow ever stronger.

Fortunately for me, André Tramble turned out to be that main brother to accompany me to Washington, D.C. I had called André to ask him about going to the March. He told me that he knew I would call him and that his answer would be yes. Isn't it interesting how "brothers" can think so much alike! God always teaches us that everything is done for a reason.

As I drove to pick up André, I was very nervous about attending the March. I felt good knowing that we would experience this powerful event. I knew that this was going to be a historic and true test presented to the African American man. After all, the entire world was watching.

As we left Cleveland heading toward the Ohio turnpike, we started to see cars with various license plates: Michigan, Indiana,

Illinois, and others. Each car was filled with Black men. The caravan that was forming was very uplifting.

After the first two hours of our trip, I decided to stop at a rest area outside Pittsburgh, Pennsylvania. As we pulled into the parking lot, we saw something unbelievable. We saw the old, the young, fathers, sons, uncles, nephews, grandfathers, and grandsons sharing and expressing love one to another. Brothers from different parts of the country also expressed greetings—greetings that would form new friendships. It was hard not to shed a tear of joy that night.

The next day, as we entered Washington, D.C., the airwaves were full of discussions about the March. We parked outside Silver Spring, Maryland, and took the Metro transit train into the capital. As we rode, we listened to some brothers talk about their thoughts on the March and what they were expecting. We all knew we were in for a memorable time. We walked toward the Mall area between the Capitol and the Washington Monument. We looked over a sea of thousands and thousands and thousands of African American men. It was a great sight to see!

During the entire day, from eleven in the morning until seven at night, we listened and spoke with brothers from all parts of the country. We talked about the speakers and their messages. One brother from New York City told us that "the March should send a clear message to everyone throughout this country that the Black man can handle his own affairs without any interference from anyone."

The Day of Atonement, which was the main reason for the Million Man March, showed that we must reaffirm our commitment to the ones who are lost. Some of our brothers have not shown respect toward their women, their wives, their children, and especially, themselves.

On our return to Cleveland, André and I talked about the issues as we saw them. But what now? Can we return to our communities with the belief that this March was our chance to show our people that the Black man still has hope? André and I believe we can and will succeed.

I hope that my reflection on the Million Man March will give someone hope. Black men are not finished. We are just getting started.

What Did It Mean?

GRANVILLE K. WHITE

It was only by the grace of God that I was off from work on October 16, 1995. This is a date that I will always remember and look forward to. It was the day of the Million Man March.

Critics said, "It couldn't be done." Others said, "No one could get that many Black males together, and if they did come together, something bad would happen." Well, guess what? The Million Man March did happen. Over a million men attended, and it was a peaceful and spiritful day.

What did the March mean to us as a people? It means we need to stop the "lip service" about "what we need to do" and just do it! It means that we, as Black men, need to set examples so that the next generation will have role models to look up to.

It means that we, as a people, need to stop waiting for others to do for us and come to grips with the reality that we need to do for ourselves. If we continue in the direction we are going, the cycle of oppression will not change.

However, in order to do these things, we, as a people, must break some traditions and taboos. First, if we believe that "sin" is the ultimate problem, then preachers and the people in the pews are going to have to leave the safety of their pulpits and sanctuaries. They must go into their communities and eradicate the sin that exists in the streets. If ministers and those who believe in a God are not willing to do this, then nothing at all is going to change.

We, as Black men, must join with them and take our communities back from drug dealers and gang-bangers. We need to go out into the streets and talk to our youth to find out where we have failed. If we were to take the time to listen to them, we might be pleasantly surprised or unpleasantly dismayed at what we heard. Before we do this, however, we need to take our rightful position in the home.

We need to start our own businesses and employ our youth. Likewise, we need to spend our monetary resources wisely and in our own communities. If we work together collectively, we would retain for some and develop for others a sense of worth and pride.

What does all of this mean? It means that once we have "made it," we should stop trying to get what some perceive to be the "prize of all prizes"—a White woman and a home in the suburbs. If we live in our communities, then younger children will have positive role models to emulate rather than drug dealers and gang-bangers.

Finally, each man needs to do something so that he can say to himself and to others, "This is what I did . . ." October sixteenth was a very important day. Those who attended the March left knowing that they had a goal to accomplish. If we do nothing to accomplish this goal, it certainly will be a crying shame.

Building a Network

STEVE H. ALEXANDER

As I reflect on October 16, 1995, I am consumed by this cultural awakening, this self-realization of who I am—who we are—and what my—our—destiny is.

As salmon are called back to their spawning ground by a supernatural force, I, along with one million other African American men, was spiritually called by a supernatural force to assemble in unity and love. We showed the world that we are men of character—men who long to reach out to our communities devastated by a drug epidemic, teen pregnancy, and the violence and self-hatred that threaten to bring our people to the brink of total destruction.

We came to repent for our apathy as Black middle-class people, and we came to atone for our indifference to the plight of the inner cities. We came to call our people back to God, to the responsibility of values that has allowed us to prosper in a land that has been hostile to us since we were kidnapped and brought here in chains over four hundred years ago.

We attended this March to say to those who control the wealth and power of this country that we may be African by descent and culture, but we are also American by birth and culture. We have borne the burden of every war, from Crispus Attucks, the first to fall in the Revolutionary War, to the Gulf War led by General Colin Powell. We have given our precious blood; the sweat of our brows; the creativity of our arts, blues, jazz; and our accomplishments in athletics to make America what it is today. We have used our inventive minds to design Washington, D.C., and street lights. We have given our precious blood to make critical discoveries in the field of medicine—including the discovery of blood plasma and its use. We have performed the first open heart surgery; and Dr. Benjamin Carson, the esteemed surgeon of Johns Hopkins University Hospital, has performed life-saving operations.

We have paid our dues to this great society—a society that we helped to build. It angers us that we must look our children in their eyes and tell them that we still are not treated like first-class citizens and that we still are not afforded first-class citizenship. What angers us even more is that we have watched European immigrants, the Italians, the Germans, the Irish, the Polish and others, come to this country—our land of sweet tears of thee—to sit at the table of economic freedom, obtain educational opportunities, get elected to the highest office of the land, and share in the great American dream, all at our expense.

People of European descent then have the gall to say, "We don't want you in our neighborhoods." "We think less of you because of the color of your skin and because of the texture of your hair." We, as African American men, have watched immigrants welcomed to the table of justice, a table that has been systematically denied to us or used against us.

My mother always told me I had to work twice as hard as my White brothers. However, I could only go half as far because of glass ceilings and racial bigotry. Nevertheless, I tell my White brothers—many of whom I attend church with, many who love me and I them—that being a Black man in this country is unprecedented. Unprecedented because on a daily basis, we as Black people face unnecessary obstacles. If we were truly to live out the words of our Constitution, that "all men are created equal and have the right to life, liberty, and the pursuit of happiness," then we would have a level playing field. Remember, no lie lives forever! Not even the Constitution. This country must evolve toward truth, justice, and liberty for all, or like all lies it will pass away.

So, what now? Rev. Jesse Jackson would say we must not become bitter but become better with the opportunities that are opened to us. We as African Americans have approximately the eighth-largest economy in the world. But we are divided. We are hoodwinked by our own stereotypes and self-hatred instead of realizing the power that we hold through economic cooperatives.

The Million Man March is our legacy. However, as great as it was, we *must not* let the spirit die. So I, Al Smith, president and cofounder, along with some of the participants in the March, started our own Million Man Network. We took a long, hard look at the ills of our community; there are many ills. But rather than being over-whelmed with the tasks, we are motivated to attack each concern, one by one. We will work hand in hand with other African American community-based programs like Know About Me (KAM), which works to uplift and edify African Americans, especially African American youths. KAM helps people to move toward self-pride, self-reliance, educational excellence, and self-employment opportunities.

We are spearheading a mentoring program with the sole purpose of teaching Black youth maturity and morally righteous living. We also are working to help our lost brothers who betray their community by poisoning it with alcohol or illegal substances. We pray we can win them over and recruit them to work for truth and justice for a new beginning in their community rather than allowing them to continue their destruction and greed. We also will be involved in voter registration drives.

We in the Million Man Network are compiling a database of people who support economic freedom. We want to invite others to cooperate with us by joining our organization to create buying power. We will go to major businesses with our large database and get discounts for all purchases from groceries to cars, knowing that part of the proceeds will be funneled back into our communities. These funds will help to support our efforts and those of other people to fight the ills of our communities. Of the approximately $347 billion dollars that African Americans control, 97 percent leaves the Black community; the money is not spent there. The Million Man Network says *no* to economic illiteracy. If we are not welcomed at the economic table with justice and fair play, let us create our own table. We will build this economic database into a powerful bargaining chip. We want our money to return to our communities so that we can build our own financial systems; rebuild technical schools; build computer schools and other state-of-the-art businesses; and train our brothers to trade in a global economy. We would then be prepared for all the new opportunities from Africa as she expands her global trade. The Pan-African diaspora is now awakening.

If you would like to be a part of this bright tomorrow, please write to Million Man Network c/o Steve Alexander, 804 London

Court, Frederick, MD 21701. To be respected in America you must have economic power, for the very foundation of a capitalistic society is economic power.

May God guide your pathway to self-actualization by becoming all that God created us to be. May God's peace always be upon you and yours. Remember, we are spiritual beings having a human experience. Let's live this experience to its fullest.

The Message and the Messenger

ANONYMOUS

The most frequently heard comment about the Million Man March is that "The message is separable from the messenger." I'm not convinced of the validity of that statement.

As the primary architect of this monumental event, the messenger has assumed, in the minds of many, Martin-like proportions. For those hungering for leadership from any corner, opposition to grossly intolerant past pronouncements of the messenger will wither under the heat of the euphoria of Black pride and connectedness generated by the March. The messenger took the initiative. He has now taken the high ground.

When there is a call to identify the person who speaks loudest for Black America, this messenger will contend for, if not occupy, the top of the list. This is the same messenger who, "in the name of truth," has refused to retract anti-Semitic statements or repudiate his anti-Christian and separatist stance. His concept of truth—which paints everyone who, by color or faith, is inimical to his claims with the same brush—is a notion that we as African Americans have always denounced.

As a demonstration of the potential for African American men to come together to affirm their divinely appointed roles as fathers, husbands, and providers, the March was an unqualified success.

The same spirit must take root in the Christian community. Christ's model of unconditional love—God's realm welcomes *all*—must be the basis for the redemption of Black men.

Belated though it may be, the March must become the clarion call for sideline Christian leaders to stand up for manliness without the shackles of rancor and blame.

The "Eyes" Have It

HUGH BRANDON

The eyes have it. The eyes of the Million Man March stand prominent in my memories of this once-in-a-lifetime experience. In the African American community, one "wrong" look can get an individual in big trouble. Historically, Black men were not allowed to look in the eyes of a White man. Black men were abused and often killed for "looking" at a White man or woman. Looking at someone, especially in their eyes, indicated that you were defiant or disrespectful. I personally believe that it indicates strength, power, and purpose.

This practice used by racist Americans years ago has carried over to the interrelationships of Black men today. Many a fight or killing has been the result of how someone "looked" at someone else.

I can recall an event that occurred one day when my eighty-three-year-old father and I sat in a crowded hospital waiting room. A young man berated my father without any provocation because he allegedly "stared" at him. How embarrassed he was when I informed him that my dad had glaucoma and was legally blind. His eyes were focused in the direction of this young man; however, he could see little, especially not his accuser.

As Black men, we have often been confronted with the words, "What are you looking at?" Well, Monday, October 16, 1995, that changed. Black men were looking at each other and it felt good. The "eyes" had it, and they held a vision and other men. Black men proudly looked at one another without suspicion or anger.

The looks given among those gathered were of concern, excitement, compassion, respect, and dignity. Tall men looked at short men. Large men looked at small men. Young men looked at old men. Christians looked at Muslims. Heterosexual men looked at homosexual men. Gang-bangers looked at nerds. Black men looked into the eyes and souls of other Black men, and it felt good.

50

I enjoyed looking at my seventeen-year-old nephew as he looked in amazement at the number of Black men gathered in preparation for the March. Early in the morning, he watched with a silent zeal as Black men came in droves to board transportation without confusion. Men packed into trains and looked at one another with heads held high. We all rejoiced in the victory of just being together. My nephew's eyes had an unbelievable glow in that early morning light.

Black men looked at each other with a newfound admiration. Brothers looked into the eyes of other brothers and saw the greatness of the "new" kings of Africa. Brothers looked out for one another. Brothers saw, felt, and knew that they were made in the image of God.

What now? On a daily basis, let's look at one another in our homes and communities with respect, compassion, and purpose. Let's not be our own oppressors by forcing one another to walk past each other with our eyes to the ground or with heads bowed in fear.

In the spirit of the Million Man March, let's look proudly into the eyes and souls of our brothers. Let's share the love we so freely gave to one another on October 16, 1995, every day of the year. It will cost very little and will produce more than money can buy.

Our Collective Responsibility

JACK SULLIVAN JR.

On October 16, 1995, I flew into Washington, D.C., after attending a meeting in Montreal, Canada. From the moment I departed the aircraft, I noticed my heart beating faster and faster as I anticipated seeing over a million brothers on the Washington Mall.

One week prior to the March, I learned that my friend who was to attend the March with me would now be unable to attend. I had to accept the fact that I would truly be "one in a million," without any realistic expectation of seeing anyone I knew in a crowd so large.

As I left the airport, I noticed scores of brothers scattered throughout the baggage claim area waiting for their luggage and limousine service to the Mall. Although I did not notice one familiar face, the brothers I encountered were very kind to me as they spoke in tones of reverent expectation. Respect, reverence, and courtesy formed the order of the day. I moved on to the subway stop, where I saw hundreds of brothers purchasing fare cards to ride the Metro to the Mall. It was during this time that I met a brother from Toledo, Ohio. He, like me, was a minister, and he, too, was traveling alone.

This brother and I did more than exchange names and business cards. We became companions for the day, listening to words of challenge and inspiration from the wise brothers and sisters who adorned the speakers' platform. My new friend and I exchanged stories about our lives, our ministries, and our ideas, as we strode through the crowd, standing on our feet for over eight hours.

The speakers reminded all of us to take seriously our roles in the establishment of healthy families, positive youth, and peaceful communities across the country. We were encouraged to return to our homes with enthusiastic commitment to volunteer in organizations that seek the positive development of our children and youth.

I enthusiastically applauded the passionate pleas directed toward African American men! Yet, perhaps the most significant experience for me on October 16 was meeting this brother from Toledo—one who acknowledged my humanity and treated me with integrity within a crowd of over a million people. We could have ignored each other, or nodded our heads at each other (as brothers often do) and continued on our way. Instead, we formed a bond that neither of us will ever forget.

In many ways, our communities have become crowds filled with faces, some more familiar than others. Neighbors often refuse to speak to one another or acknowledge the humanity of others. Too many brothers carry and use arms of destruction and death. How sad. Yet, I am convinced that the health and wholeness we desire so strongly for our communities are inextricably tied to our ability to affirm the humanity and integrity of each person in our communities.

We cannot afford the perverse luxury of adhering to policies and lifestyles that alienate and scapegoat huge portions of our communities. It is our collective responsibility to recognize one another's dignity, no matter how large the crowd becomes. These affirmations are not to be done uncritically. As we acknowledge the God-given worth of all segments of our communities, we must find the courage to spend our time and our money in ways that can enhance the lives of persons in our neighborhoods and beyond.

So then, let us resolve that we will shake off the shackles of market-driven "rugged individualism" in exchange for the beloved community, which seeks an atmosphere of justice and love—an atmosphere with ideas and resources being shared for the common good. Brothers, let us resolve that we will renounce the use of arms designed to instill fear and inflict violence, and instead use our human arms to spread caring and promote healing across our communities.

We did it on October 16; we can do it every day. I know we can! Thank God for the Million Man March. And for my brother from Toledo. Amen.

We Owe Our Very Best

RICHARD A. ROWE

The Million Man March was truly a historic and remarkable event. Those of us who were blessed and fortunate to be at the March will never forget what we saw, heard, or experienced. Never! The March was not only a day for atonement, but it became, for many of us, a pilgrimage—a return to our sanity, decency, and nobility.

The weather was perfect, the atmosphere was peaceful, and the brotherhood was powerful. Great-grandfathers, grandfathers, fathers, uncles, cousins, sons, and grandsons of African ancestry affectionately affirmed one another's presence. We were, at least for that one day, our "brothers' keepers." The spirit of "He ain't heavy, he's my brother" permeated the air. The souls of Black men were on display. And behold, it was an extraordinarily peaceful demonstration—full of compassion, commitment, and community.

The March marked the beginning of a movement, where men of African ancestry viewed themselves not as victims, but rather as problem solvers who must accept personal responsibility for their actions and destinies. Furthermore, each man in attendance pledged to honor, respect, and love Black women, Black children, and one another.

They also pledged to return to their communities and join and/ or support Black organizations, churches, newspapers, and businesses. Consequently, those of us who attended the March now understand that we can never return to "business as usual." The stakes are too high and the task at hand is too great.

A few years ago, a myriad of reports and studies on the Black male concluded with substantial statistical evidence that Black men were on a collision course with disaster. The studies further suggested Black men viewed themselves as victims who were defeated, downtrodden, and dejected by the "system." There would never be any peace or bright tomorrow for the Black man. He would re main a pathological psychopath to be hunted, maligned, arrested, incarcerated, and, if necessary, killed.

As a result of internalizing these defeatist messages, Black men began to abandon their children, abuse their women, and engage in self-/group-destructive behaviors. In essence, they "lost their way."

Far too many Black men read these reports and quickly succumb to a memory lapse. They forget to recall the Black pride of Marcus Garvey, the vast intellectual wisdom of W. E. B. DuBois, or the political savvy of Booker T. Washington and Frederick Douglass. Furthermore, they forget Malcolm's discipline, Martin King's endurance, Medgar's courage, and the power and spirit of the countless men and women of yesteryear.

The Million Man March reminded all in attendance that they must never forget from "whence they came." It reminded us that we must recapture, reclaim, and reaffirm the high level of discipline, commitment, courage, sacrifice, and personal excellence that our ancestors displayed and practiced despite the odds. "Never give up," "Now is the time," "Believe in God," and "Up, you mighty race" were some of the daily mantras that kept African Americans during the civil rights movement looking up and keeping their eyes on the prize.

And now, as we move closer to the first-year celebration of the great Million Man March, it would surely be a tragedy if every person who was of voting age had not registered to vote; or joined an organization or a church; or attended a PTA/PTO meeting; or reached out to another person; or signed up as a mentor for a younger person; or committed at least 25 percent of his or her consumer dollars to Black-owned businesses; or subscribed to a Black magazine; or initiated a self-, family-, or community-uplift effort; or sought treatment/help for destructive addictions of any kind. If we have yet to hug and spend a few more hours with our children, or to make our wives/mates feel special and loved, then we have failed to hear the message or heed the warning from the March.

If we have done all of the above, great. If we have done one or two of the aforementioned, we should start feeling better about ourselves. However, if we as serious African American men have yet to begin or act, then we have no right to enter the twenty-first century. For those of us who have begun the "action phase" called forth from the March, I would suggest that we do the following:

1. Place God/Creator first in our lives.
2. Place a picture of the Million Man March and pledge on a special wall in our homes and touch/read it every day.
3. Pray.
4. Prepare a daily self-improvement plan and stick to it.
5. Practice saying these two words every day: "I can."
6. Pray.
7. Promise to reach out to one other brother and share the pledge with him.
8. Pledge to pursue personal excellence in everything we do.
9. Provide sufficient time for family life.
10. Pray.

The choice is ours, and we owe our ancestors, our children, our women, and God our very best. "If God be for us, who can be against us?" Peace.

Something Happened

AMOTI NYABONGO

My life in the United States has been relatively uneventful. I was born and raised in Brooklyn, New York. As a preteen, I remember the sixties being very turbulent. My mother and family did their best to shield me and my siblings from what was going on (the Harlem riots, the assassination of Malcolm X, etc.) and gave me and my cousins what they felt was a good home environment and upbringing.

Things started to change when I became a teenager. I attended an inner-city high school during the era of being Black and proud. In keeping with my peers, I wore my hair in the Afro style, which was funny because my father was African.

As a young Black male in New York City in the seventies, there were many disadvantages. During this era, our film and literary heroes were pimps or drug dealers. We bought all the fashions to look the part of our "heroes." This had some interesting consequences for most of my friends. It made us easier targets for the police, but that's another story.

Unexpectedly, one day in 1975, something happened. I heard a man preach Black pride on the radio. He pointed out the real enemy of African Americans. His name was Louis Farrakhan. He was different. His message was different, and his people were different. They dressed conservatively. I was too young to resonate with Malcolm X and barely remember Martin Luther King Jr. However, I listened to many broadcasts delivered by the man named Louis Farrakhan.

During this period, the war in Vietnam had ended and I was attending college. My school was packed with returning veterans. They had returned with the understanding that life is precious, fragile, and short. They knew tomorrow was not promised, and it showed in everything they did.

For the most part, I watched in silence, occasionally talking with them when we had a class together. The message that everyone seemed to relay was "Have a goal and make it happen." So I did. I transferred to a historically Black college in the South and set out to achieve my goal.

In the summer of 1978, I saw Louis Farrakhan speak. Now with new understanding, he was speaking to me. When I returned to school that fall, I took my first Black history course. It was there that I was introduced to Malcolm X. That was almost twenty years ago.

As you can see, my life was uneventful. Uneventful, until October, 16, 1995. Until that Monday my experiences were my own.

I headed to Washington, D.C., on Sunday, the day before the March. As I traveled down the New Jersey Turnpike, I saw buses, vans, and carloads of Black men heading to Washington. License plates on cars read Maine, Massachusetts, Vermont, and Connecticut. Inside, men were waving, giving the peace sign or their respective lodge or fraternity sign. In Maryland, where state troopers are known for pulling over speeders, someone must have issued a directive regarding vehicles occupied by Black men. I didn't see one car or van with Black occupants being pulled over.

I spent the night with one of my closest fraternity brothers. One of his coworkers stopped by before we turned in for the night. There was a van pool available to get to the March, but it was leaving at 4:45 A.M. in order to arrive in time for the dawn prayer service.

At 4:30 A.M. we were up. Thirty minutes later we were on the Mall. It was still dark, but there were portable halogen lamps to provide light. The crisp morning air was scented with incense, and in the distance one could hear the sound of ceremonial drums. Even at that early hour, the Mall was crowded. The steps to the Capitol building were packed. Black men from everywhere and all walks of life arrived every second, bringing their spirit to the collective.

The day was very spiritual. I could feel the love, the respect, the warmth, and the compassion transcending one to another. The words "thank you," "excuse me," "pardon me," "please," "take care," "peace," and "stay strong" echoed across the Mall as we made our way through the crowd.

I thought I would run into old friends, but there were just too many people. I did run across one friend from college. We shared a few words, but for the most part we were speechless. Personally, I had too much to say, too much to ask, and too little time.

The day was long, with a lot to take in. The guest speakers, the individual conversations, the picture taking, and networking were all a part of the day. People were overwhelmed by the magnitude of the spirit that was present.

Will it happen again? I can't say. For those who attended, we need to keep the spirit we experienced alive. We need to pass it on every chance we get. The March was a rejuvenating event for me. On this one day, I felt at home and at peace.

October 16, 1995, began a new experience in my life—a life that had once been uneventful, but now changed forever.

Called Out

RONALD COOK

On a warm October morning in 1995, a silent army marched down a street in Washington, D.C. Walking. Shoulders straight. Heads lifted. Eyes focused. They marched. The marchers said nothing, no singing or shouting, no protest songs. Just silence as they marched toward the Capitol.

The clear crystal skies and radiant sun added just the right touch to the amazing army moving briskly toward the Capitol. The cheers from the many spectators along the road strengthened the silent army as they marched proudly.

> If my people who are called by my name humble themselves, pray, seek my face, and turn from their wicked ways, then I will hear from heaven, and will forgive their sin and heal their land. (2 Chron. 7:14)

"If my people who are called by my name humble themselves." This was the reason the army came to Washington, D.C. Called out as the people of God to humble themselves, pray, and turn from their wicked ways. This army wanted to hear from God for the healing of the land. The Million Man March was a real affirmation that the Black male wants to confront the question that plagues the African American community, "Is the African American male an endangered species?"

The March was one of the greatest experiences in my life, surrounded by hundreds of thousands of men from all over the world, standing together, united as one body, helping one another, caring and sharing with one another. We embraced one another for the first time and shed tears of joy in our oneness. Never in the history of humankind have so many humans gathered at one time for the same purpose—to covenant to save our people and the Black male from extinction.

Our presence was a confirmation to the world that we are "alive" and united and that we are called out as God's children to pray, to seek forgiveness, and to atone for our sins. We are also to organize within our communities, our families, our religious institutions, businesses, schools, economic development organizations, all under the guidance of God.

On that unforgettable day in October, I was so proud to be a Black male in America. The invisible force that moved throughout the day, from man to man, from child to child, became visible as the day ended. We hugged one another. The feeling of many showed that this was the first time they had ever really embraced their brothers in a positive, affectionate, affirming, reassuring, and genuine spirit of kinship.

As I reflect on the events of that day, my heart begins to race, my eyes get misty, and my spirit seems to jump just thinking of the pure joy of being alive to take part in the event.

The pastor of my church decided to take part in the March. He had the church charter a bus to take some of the men from our weekly food pantry and from our homeless project to the March. He wanted to give these men an opportunity to be a part of this event, knowing that it could be a life-changing experience for some of them.

On the night we departed, the evidence of what my pastor expected began to take shape. The men began to see something real in the people of God. Church members donated food and beverages, and they also donated clothes. Every man who signed up to go, could attend. At first, my pastor was not going to attend the March. Something changed his mind. He, along with two or three deacons, traveled to Washington, D.C., on the bus. We prayed and sang songs of faith as we headed to Washington.

This silent army was composed of many individuals from all walks of life. Many of them had one thing in common, "broken spirits." These men came together as one body to help to heal some of these broken spirits, hearts, families, hopes, and dreams.

We did not go to Washington as an army to wage war or to protest to the government; we did not go to stage boycotts or threaten government leaders for change. We gathered as African American males to renew our strength, find our paths for the future, and covenant with one another. Because we do and will have a future.

God has given each human being the free will to be a positive force for change. We are blessed to be a blessing as children of God. The color of a person's skin does not measure the quality of his or her character, or the size of his or her heart to love. The African American male is somebody. He is a child of God, blessed with life to be whatever he strives to be, if he calls upon God for guidance.

The Million Man March was a living testimony to the world that we, as African American males, can come together in silence, in prayer, in love, harmony, peace, and joy. We are disciplined, respectful, obedient, and we have a concern for the future of our race.

We asked God to forgive us our past sins against our families, communities, and ourselves. We committed ourselves to work together to rebuild our communities, our families, and one another.

We prayed together as one family for our survival, our women, and our children. We asked God to give us strength to be the respected heads of the house and leaders in the community.

Prayer

God, we thank you that we are called by your name. We bless your name for the gift of life. We confess that we often have fallen short of what you would have us do with the free will you have given us. We thank you for your presence in Washington, D.C., and the life-changing experiences for those present and those who could not attend. We pray that you will hear our prayers and heal our land. Amen.

❷

❸

⑤

⑥

❽

❾

U.N.I.A.-A.C.L.
WOODSON-BANNEKER
DRUMBEAT · HERITAGE GALLERY INT'L
AFRICAN FREEDOM FUND TREASURY
DIVISION 330

1. *The Capitol Mall, Washington, D.C.* Photo © 1995 Rick Reinhard / Impact Visuals.

2. *"Black men standing tall, unbent, and unbowed."* Photo © 1995 Rick Reinhard / Impact Visuals.

3. *One of the Fruit of Islam.* Photo © 1995 Christopher Smith / Impact Visuals.

4. *Nation of Islam leader Louis Farrakhan addressing the March.* Photo © 1995 Jay Mallin / Impact Visuals.

5. *Marchers registering to vote.* Photo © 1995 Rick Reinhard / Impact Visuals.

6. *Young men attending the March.* Photo © 1995 Jetta Fraser / Impact Visuals.

7. *March organizer Benjamin Chavis speaking to the press before the March.* Photo © 1995 Christopher Smith / Impact Visuals.

8. Photo © 1995 Jetta Fraser / Impact Visuals.

9. Photo © 1995 Christopher Smith / Impact Visuals.

10. Photo © 1995 Christopher Smith / Impact Visuals.

Seize the Time

SILAS NORMAN JR.

I am a former civil rights worker. My last formal assignment was as the Alabama State Director for the Student Non-violent Coordinating Committee (SNCC).

I am not given to marching. I purposefully did not attend the 1963 March on Washington and enthusiastically supported SNCC's official decision not to participate in the Selma to Montgomery march in 1965.

As I started to pay attention to the call by Minister Louis Farrakhan for a Million Man March on Washington and listened to traditional enemies and detractors of progress in the African American community, I became convinced that the October 16 March had become more than a march.

I viewed it as a challenge to Black manhood and self-determination and an opportunity for us to unify and take charge of our communities and lives. How dare they tell me I should not respond to Minister Farrakhan! One can say whatever one will about the Nation of Islam. They have earned the right to represent the aspirations of our race. They have rescued our young men from drugs, jails, and despair. They have modeled a discipline that has brought dignity and respect to its adherents.

I didn't know if we would have a million men, but something compelled me to go. I was distressed that our traditional Black leadership was not supporting the March; some were even speaking against it. But I also did not know that more than a million African American men from all socioeconomic and political persuasions also had come independently to a decision that they would participate in the March.

A few traditional leaders did recognize the mood of Black men and became involved late in the preparation for the March. It was a positive sign that even a few of these leaders joined the March.

Prior to our departure, the staging area in Detroit was to be a microcosm of what it would be like on the day of the March. The Million Man March was a powerful, peaceful, and impressive gathering of men and women. Some actually marched by land over long distances. Some came by plane and rail, and others came in an array of buses and cars. All added to the feeling of pride and hope that energized those present. It would prove to be a more powerful spiritual experience than I had ever imagined possible.

The drama continued to build as we gathered at our staging area in Maryland and made our way to Washington via the Metro trains. When we arrived at the March site at approximately 7 A.M., several hundred thousand men and women were already assembled. There was a real sense of history and unity in the disciplined atmosphere. Most of us stood with little concern for personal comfort through Minister Farrakhan's address, which lasted several hours and ended about 6 P.M.

Minister Farrakhan's address was long and was not delivered in the fiery style of skilled Black orators. However, most marchers and I listened intently to every word. It was one of the most powerful addresses I have ever heard. It was historically and spiritually challenging and conciliatory to all detractors.

I am encouraged that a few more of our traditional leaders have been able to overcome their reservations. Likewise, I appreciate the willingness of the average Black man to take an interest in his own destiny.

We left Washington as peacefully as we had come, having conducted ourselves with dignity and resolve. We left the city as clean as we had found it. Only God could have called such a gathering. I am a Christian by birth, upbringing, and conviction, but I know that God can call whomever God chooses to do the divine will. God chose Minister Farrakhan for this moment in history. I am grateful.

We have a lot of work to do. I am not surprised that our organizational infrastructure is not in place or finely enough tuned to follow up appropriately on all of the challenges and possibilities that were placed before us. But I do know that we returned with a resolve and spiritual strength to cooperate more; to develop our spiritual strength; to be better men, husbands, fathers, and contributors to our women, our families, and our communities.

The Million Man March, which was supported directly and indirectly by many women, has the possibility of being a major transformative milestone in the history of our people. All we have to do is seize the time. We shall overcome!

Poised for a Revolution

TODD L. LEDBETTER

When I arrived in the Washington, D.C., area on October 8, 1993, I didn't know what to expect. I came looking for a new beginning. I came hoping for new and exciting opportunities. I was fortunate to have traveled many different places, both in the United States and abroad. However, the city of Pittsburgh, Pennsylvania, was the only home I had known for all of my twenty-seven years. It was time for a change. I considered New York and Atlanta; but ultimately, I settled on and in Chocolate City, USA—Washington, D.C.

Living in Washington has indeed afforded me some interesting opportunities: the opportunity to interact with some of the best and brightest of my people; the opportunity to work with youth in Washington's inner city; the opportunity to worship in one of the most progressive and dynamic churches in the nation; the opportunity to study (albeit briefly) at one of the most prestigious historically Black institutions of higher learning; and the opportunity to witness from ground zero the coming together of one of the most significant events in our history—the Million Man March.

A few months before my move, I came to Washington for the thirtieth anniversary March on Washington. Born nearly three years after the 1963 March, I saw this as an opportunity to experience some of the spirit and energy that I had missed the first time. I left the event disappointed. One of my great disappointments was that Minister Louis Farrakhan, who was scheduled to speak, was asked at the last minute not to attend.

My disappointment grew further when I read a flyer handed to me by a member of the Nation of Islam. It was a copy of a fax sent to the event's organizing committee by David Sapperstein of the Anti-Defamation League, admonishing, almost warning the organizers not to include Farrakhan in the march. I was disgusted to learn that the agenda of an event whose leadership and mandate were predominantly African American could be altered from outsiders at the drop of a fax.

It soon became clear that I was not alone in my indignation. In the following days, "mainstream" Black leadership reached out to Minister Farrakhan. The Congressional Black Caucus invited him to speak at its annual legislative conference. March organizers conceded that excluding him was "a mistake." The inflammatory words of Nation of Islam minister Khalid Abdul Muhammed caused some of the outreach efforts to back off, but the die had been cast: Black folks were tired of being dictated to by forces external to the African American community.

When the Million Man March was announced, a lot of people didn't know what to make of it. Some were indifferent, some skeptical. Others were hostile. And as amazing as it seems now, the mainstream media almost completely ignored it—consumed as they were with the O. J. Simpson trial. House Speaker Newt Gingrich seemed totally unaware of the event even when confronted with a question about the March at a D.C. town meeting in August of 1995.

Fortunately, Black media personalities in Washington, D.C., like Cathy Hughes and Bob Law, got behind the Million Man March. Progressive Black Christian ministers, like my pastor, the Reverend Willie F. Wilson, also supported the March. A buzz grew in the Black community, and as it became clear that the March *was* going to happen, detractors surfaced.

In addition to familiar cries of "anti-Semitism," mainstream media outlets rounded up every African American of any repute who opposed the March, from Angela Davis to Armstrong Williams. I had conversations with people who opposed the March solely because of Farrakhan.

One coworker went so far as to call him an "Antichrist" and to speak of being "unevenly yoked," claiming that Farrakhan didn't have Jesus in his heart. In a meeting, another coworker, who is White, ignorantly asserted that Farrakhan was "calling for a riot." I quickly and pointedly cleared up his misconceptions.

My cousin, who is like a brother to me and with whom I share a house, even expressed serious reservations about the March, largely because his pastor was opposed to it. The Bible was frequently invoked in opposition to the March. However, Scripture also says that the righteous may be identified by their fruits and that "the rocks shall cry out" if no one else will.

I pondered all of the arguments, pro and con. I concluded that with the epidemic of physical, mental, and spiritual decay in our communities, if this March would cause some or our people to think more deeply, act more responsibly, if only for one day, then God's will be done. If the March would be the beginning of a process whereby we could begin to proactively address the issues that have plagued our communities for so long, who in their right mind could possibly be against it?

Many of the voices arrayed against the March, pastors in particular, could have called such an event themselves. So why didn't they? Is their opposition legitimate concern or petty jealousy?

The day of the March was picture-perfect. Midweek predictions of rain gave way to a beautiful, clear, sunny autumn day. I was dizzy with anticipation as I emerged from the Archives-Navy Memorial Metro station. "I'm here. It's really happening." For the first half-hour, I asked everyone I saw wearing a Pittsburgh Steelers jacket, "You from Pittsburgh?" "Yeah." "So am I. I live here now." "Oh yeah? What part you from? . . ."

I was happy to see the hometown so well represented. I met brothers from other places—New York, Chicago, Los Angeles, Florida, the Carolinas, New Orleans. They made way for each other and helped each other up the wall behind the Capitol reflecting pool. Ordinarily I would be wary and guarded in such a large crowd, but there was to be none of that this day. There we stood, cheering Rosa Parks, weeping along with Maya Angelou. One brother from California passed around a book, asking brothers to sign, "for his grandchildren."

Total unity and singularity of purpose prevailed—a unity that would have been limited had there been more women present. There was none of the "fronting" or distraction that we, in our incompleteness, fall into over our sisters. Most of the women who were there were working either for the March or other organizations.

Some registered people to vote, or attended with husbands, fathers, boyfriends, and families.

The television footage I saw later that day was amazing. People, beautiful people, stretching as far as the eye or camera could see. A living sea of Blackness.

In the aftermath of the March, there was a spirit, a glow that stayed with the participants for days, even weeks. There were reports of people being more courteous in their cars and on the streets. Detroit's infamous "Devil's Night" arson spree didn't happen, thanks to the nearly twenty thousand men who stood up in the spirit of the Million Man March.

All over the country, there was the sense that we had really done something. You knew that you had been a part of history. Even those who originally opposed it—including Black "conservatives" such as Armstrong Williams and Robert Woodson—have had to change their tune.

My White coworker came to me and apologized, stating that the March was an impressive event, and that even though he still didn't like Farrakhan, he "couldn't find fault with anything he had to say." Thankfully my cousin did attend the March, persuaded by the fact that his father and brother traveled all the way from Detroit to take part. There are ongoing disputes about the numbers of people in attendance: Most mainstream publications still will not give full credit for the million-plus men in attendance; most cite a figure of eight hundred thousand. Additionally, there was a dispute about the money that was collected before and during the March. Despite this, the March was, by any definition, a success.

The greatest beneficiary of this success may be the Black church. Forced to confront itself, will the church shake off the vestiges of enslavement theology and respond with new fervor to the economic, political, social, and cultural demands of the community? It is clear that the pressure to become more culturally relevant has impacted most churches in the Black nation.

From Kente cloth choir robes to references to Jesus as "the African Hebrew Messiah," the African Christian church in America is poised on the verge of revolution: to celebrate our faith in the fullness of our African culture; to manifest the power of God as Black children of God; to "Let our light so shine among people that they may see our good works, and glorify our God in heaven. Traditionalists may balk. Our White would-be spiritual overseers may warn us of the dangers of "African paganism"—itself an oxymoron. But the church must transcend the forces of reaction and resist the false security of narrow-mindedness to realize the goal of a truly holistic ministry: ministering to the needs of people in the here and now as well as the hereafter.

Any political or economic efforts toward liberation and judgmental societal justice that negate or minimize the power of the spirit are doomed to failure. This predominantly Christian people is looking for leadership and stewardship. If they don't get it from the National Baptist Convention, the Church of God in Christ, or the African Methodist Episcopal Church, they will look elsewhere. And they should.

Minister Farrakhan was called on to do a job that perhaps no one else at the time could do. You don't have to like or agree with him, but in fairness, give credit where credit is due. Also keep in mind, the March was not about Farrakhan. He, like me, like all of us, was one in a million.

When they came to Washington, D.C., on October 16, 1995, many didn't know what to expect. They came looking for a new beginning. They came hoping for new and exciting possibilities. They traveled from many places, both in the United States and abroad. They knew it was time for a change. They settled on and in Chocolate City, USA, and shook the world.

Unity of the Spirit

NATHANIEL MARTIN

On October 16, 1995, in the nation's capital, history was made. For on this day, the largest assembly of African American men in these great United States attended a celebration of spiritual renewal and a Day of Atonement. It was a great historic day in America, as Black men from all over the world put aside their biases and spiritual differences to show unity, to reconcile, and more profoundly to begin implementing a proactive social agenda or social vision for African Americans.

African Americans were drawn by Minister Louis Farrakhan's request for pride, responsibility, and action. It is doubtful that the March would ever have come to fruition without his determination. Minister Farrakhan articulated the concept all across the country. He planted in the minds of African Americans that something as grandiose and inspiring as a "Million Man March" could become a reality.

There was indeed a spirit moving through him, the focal point being the idea that time is of the essence. The untold story of the "Million Man March" is that of people rising above adversity, doubt, personal and ideological differences to make history. Minister Farrakhan advocated for African Americans to return home and join an organization, any organization, working on behalf of "Black folks." There were many obstacles that had to be overcome. Many were.

Volunteers, leaders, and individuals organizing in the trenches within many neighborhoods across this country are responsible for the great success of the Million Man March. As a testimony to this magnificent event of a million-plus men, not one negative incident was reported.

It would be a great success if only a small percentage of the men who attended the March returned home and did something for their

71

families and / or their communities. A spirit of love, brotherhood, respect, sharing, and bonding will forever be a part of their souls as well as mine.

October 16, 1995, will go down in history as the day when African American men set aside their differences and divisions for the betterment of humankind. It should also be pointed out that this spectacular event was supported, paid for, and sponsored by African Americans.

Finally, there was a bond and a feeling of "unity of the spirit" that existed between those in attendance and those who, unfortunately, could not be in attendance. The positive effects in the African American community will be felt for many years to come. The untold legacy of the Million Man March is that it was truly an uplifting spiritual day of atonement!

Yours in the bond.

A Black Man Who Loves
Black Men's Eyes

CLEO MANAGO

The eve of an unparalleled epoch. Air electric with nervous enthusiasm, in anticipation of the unknown in America: a day of national reckoning for Black men. This time, it was not just a holiday
set-aside approved by an ambivalent Congress, but a day independently seized by Black men in America. Self-determination at its
prime. It's on! A day of reconciliation—the Million Man March.

In the final hours before this Day of Atonement, in a last-ditch
effort to perplex, to douse this unmitigated flame, news reports focused on Minister Louis Farrakhan, the March's convener. CNN,
ABC, NBC, CBS, MTV, and other high-tech hypnotists posing as
"our" press amply served listeners their prime-time fare. At the
speed of light, ear-burning, sound-bitten fragments of Minister
Farrakhan's speeches were spewed forth, shaping America (and
the Western world) for a contemptuous perspective on Farrakhan's
"controversial" leadership, and the fateful day "he" had made—
October 16, 1995.

Evening television was filled with news reports instantly replay-
ing Minister Farrakhan in slow motion, in arm-waving gesture, in
a chin-holding grimace. His voice reverberated through generous
sound effects, juxtaposed with the faceless voices of White men who
"freely" provided the narrative. Minister Farrakhan's exaggerated
inflections (as if exaggeration were necessary) rumbled through
small TV speakers, magnified, uncontexualized. For the hearing
impaired or those who just didn't get it the first time, "his" words
were echoed with eye-piercing text displayed fully across the screen.

The mainstream media, though absent for the eight months prior
to the announcement of the March, at the event's twilight, jumped
aboard to portray the March's visionary as a hate-monger who calls
Jews blood-suckers, a misogynist, a hateful militant Black leader

lustfully prepared to lure a million Black men into hating White people.

Concerned voices in the community—most of whom agreed that something is needed to alter the tumultuous states of too many Black men—whispered, wondered, and worried about the safety of a million Black men in D.C. Some also questioned just how many men would be "man" enough to show up.

Rushing for the street en route to history, a last-minute phone call came in from a brother already in D.C. who worked closely with March organizers. He called to inform me that I was selected to speak at the March on behalf of same-gender-loving and bisexual Black people. I had to get there! Moved, I was temporarily disoriented, pacing, crying, nervous, soon to be among a community of brothers, knowing so well our struggle, how we suffer, how we long for a change.

The day had arrived. Early morning, Washington's great Mall lent witness to a stunning garden of Black brothers (and a few sisters), undoubtedly a million-plus strong. Consolidating, communicating, anticipating, congregating, embracing, in droves on America's Capitol grounds. Grounds built centuries ago by men of African descent, their bodies sold and beaten here, who probably could never imagine a day like today.

Yet centuries later, Black men appeared there, still captive by their search and hunger for answers, direction, affection, protection from a hurt often too abstract to mention. This pain would soon be addressed.

From the peak at the base of the African obelisk-styled Washington Monument, rows of brothers could be seen sprinkled en masse, bouncing off sunlight, brother to brother, along the three-mile stretch to the Capitol stairs. We greeted each other warmly. With welcome relief, a connection that waded just below the surface of our pain, we kissed, hugged, and smiled. Hopeful, we held each other while Maya Angelou, Dr. Maulana Karenga, Jesse Jackson, Dr. Betty Shabazz, Dick Gregory, Stevie Wonder, Marion Barry, Minister Louis Farrakhan, among others, fed us, contextualized our confusion, cultivated our humanity, equipped us with tools to carry on.

As they spoke, I walked among the swarming multitude of Black male eagerness. I was recognized by several of my brothers, who waved or greeted me. Soon I came upon a "gay Black" contingency, decked with pink triangles, gay pride placards, and gay rainbow flag cutouts of the African continent. I noticed among them a smattering of White, apparently gay men. Standing out more than this were two Black brothers face to face, tenderly embracing as if they loved each other. Onlookers not with the contingency gawked at this sight.

The Black-on-Black male couple, in close proximity to the crowd, appeared unstirred by their audience. Proudly they caressed each other, for each other and the Million Man March to receive. Men embracing had become a part of the event's landscape. Given the gay pride signs and T-shirts, it was clear that these two went beyond "brotherly love." Still, the legion of brothers in the vicinity were respectful. Not a harsh word was exchanged.

What did appear more peculiar, the gay contingency was the only Black group present with its flag held high by a White man. It was the only group whose images of pride were steeped in White-dominated ethos (i.e., White gay rainbow flags and pink German triangles). Still it was important to witness same-gender-loving brothers among the Million Man March. And we yet have much to teach and to learn.

I would later be told that I, and other, better-known speakers, would not address the crowd. This was reported as a last-minute decision based on time and priority factors. I had mixed feelings about the announcement, figuring a great opportunity to acknowledge our diversity was squelched. On the other hand, I wondered how appropriate it would have been to address a group of Black men equally marginalized, heartbroken, facing a bastion of crucial dilemmas, with issues of sexuality, maleness, and its diversity in our community—on this day.

Unified, captivated, we listened to Minister Farrakhan's keynote address. Speaking from a bulletproof glass platform, he suggested we adopt a brother in prison; register eight others to vote; and that we never use violence or weapons against anyone, except in self-defense. He suggested that we support and build Black business, and that we love and be respectful of one another. Minister Farrakhan spoke earnestly on what we understood and knew, the problem of White supremacy and its ruthless goal to dominate us and the world.

Over a million men stood enthralled, in resonance with the speaker's message. Minister Louis Farrakhan, the only man in the universe to unite over a million Black men, wept in the joy that he called, and we came. Near the evening's end, he asked that we hold hands, that we say to one another, "I love you," apologize for ever hurting one another, and that we embrace. And we did.

A sea of tears welled up in our eyes. Some were hesitant to let each other go, to let go of this moment. At Minister Farrakhan's last word, the Day of Atonement was over.

Voices of the Past

RODNEY FRANKLIN

Movements have a way of summoning voices of the past—voices that remind us of why we are here and what we are charged to do. The voices of our forebears remind us of the phenomenal contribution they made to early civilization. Those strong chords of hope resonated during slavery. Sweet words of freedom continued to be heard as the voices of our people grew stronger and stronger, heeding a call from the past during the civil rights movement.

The Million Man March was a continuation of that movement. The call for men to come to the nation's capital in solidarity was a soulful renewal. Men journeyed from the South, North, East, and West. Working men. Men looking for work. Men looking for hope. College students. Little boys with their fathers. Men of different religious backgrounds, but with one purpose—to be renewed.

The renewal began on that beautiful Monday in October as the sun splashed its radiance and kissed the faces of African American men. The renewal will only continue if we hear the voices of the past and act in new ways. One way in which we can act is for men to communicate with and mentor to each other. We must go beyond the hidden rhetoric of football, basketball, and baseball, and communicate feelings.

We need to tell of the hurt that drives us to self-destruction—destruction by way of temporary release through alcohol and other abused substances. There is no panacea for these methods. But we can begin to share and break down those walls of noncommunication by trusting and telling what's going on in our lives. When we really work in the area of communication, we will feel the renewal that can be a transformation in our lives.

We can further find renewal through mentoring. The Egyptians use a term, "*sbyoet*," which means instructions or teachings. These instructions were created nearly twenty-five hundred years before the birth of Jesus Christ. The instructions were popular and used in their community for guidance and moral teachings.

We can use *sbyoet* for renewal by linking men in various ages together. This process will assist people so that they can have a guide to direct them in helping themselves and rebuilding their communities. Mentoring relationships can be assets for renewal as we seek to hear the voices of the past.

Finally, we must be committed to supporting organizations in our communities that are designed to uplift our race. It may be easy to give lip service or write a check to help an organization, but we must go further. We need to increase the number of African American men volunteers. We need men to tutor, cook, feed, build, and actively work in their communities and in organizations.

When we have begun to communicate, develop mentoring relationships, and support organizations in our communities, the voices from the past will help us to sing the songs of freedom. Victory for our communities and for ourselves will be won!

Phi Beta Sigma
Answers the Call!

LAWRENCE E. MILLER

The Million Man March in Washington, D.C., will undoubtedly go down in history as one of the greatest events in the history of the United States. It wasn't just the million people who came from around the world to attend the March. It wasn't only the millions who listened or watched the event on radio or television. It wasn't just the thousands of Black vendors, or speakers, or those who felt, "I Am Someone Special Today—A Caring Black Man." October 16, 1995, was all these things, and so much more. It was absolutely wonderful!

The international headquarters of Phi Beta Sigma Fraternity, where I am the national executive director, was used as the headquarters for the Million Man March and the National African American Leadership Summit. For this, we were proud. Phi Beta Sigma Fraternity, Inc., has always been in the forefront of the civil rights movement, beginning in 1934 with our social action programs.

Over a thousand members of Phi Beta Sigma Fraternity, Inc., came from all across the United States to support our fraternity brother, Dr. Benjamin F. Chavis, and to say thank you to him and Minister Louis Farrakhan for having enough courage, love, and concern for our people to take the leadership.

It was a beautiful day, and hundreds of thousands of African American men came to the city in a spirit of solidarity and unity. As we reached out for a new spirit, a new attitude, and a new mind, we created a new spirit that will always be remembered and appreciated by our African American sisters. While the March was designed for men, our Nubian queens (sisters) were beautifully welcomed and greeted.

One thing I will always remember from this momentous event is that each African American man must look into his own heart, mind, and soul, and be responsible for his family, his brother, his women, and his children, and be a leader within his community.

As salaam alaikum.

A Day That Would Not Turn Me Loose!

WENDELL HARRISON FITZGERALD PHILLIPS

When I first heard about the Million Man March, I must admit, I was the least bit concerned. I just would not believe that what was supposed to occur could actually be accomplished. As much as I wanted to be a part of something momentous with regard to humanity in general, and my people in particular, the Million Man March was not the venue I would choose. But it would not "turn me loose"!

I tried to dismiss the March as another grandiose, self-promoting vehicle for some of our leaders, or just another chance for each to plug their own cause. No matter how much I tried to dismiss the March, it would not dismiss me. It would not turn me loose!

I attended the twentieth anniversary of the March on Washington. It was indeed a blessing to be at that March with my father. However, the spirit of that March was not quite right. I remember my father saying, "Martin, I'm only here out of respect for you!" Brothers were blasting their boom boxes, people were getting high, others were "fussin' and cussin'" each other.

All of what had occurred at the anniversary of the March on Washington helped to mold my cocoon of cynicism that I am still working every day to shed. I therefore believed that the Million Man March was to be just another weak chapter in a long and disappointing book. But, still, it would not turn me loose!

While I believe those who planned the anniversary March meant well, there was no real agenda. The March lacked a significant agenda because a vast number of us were still "asleep." We were still dreaming on "I Have a Dream." This is by no means a slap in Dr. King's face. I believe that the steps he took and the words he spoke were extremely necessary for the nationwide visualization of what Black America demanded. However, times have changed since the 1960s.

We were fighting the same ugly monster, but we were having a tough time finding it. All we could find were its tracks. We knew there was no racism because we had jobs—we just couldn't get promoted. We knew there was no racism because we could now vote—but the political system was corrupt, so we didn't vote. We knew there could be no racism because we could buy homes—we just could not choose where our home would be located. So, how could the Million Man March make a difference? Nevertheless, no matter how many times or ways I posed that question, it would not turn me loose!

As years passed like hours, things started to get clearer. The monster felt so comfortable with our apathy and confusion that it felt no need to disguise itself. It started to rear its ugly head—Rodney King and the acquittal of the Los Angeles police. The picture became very clear when that verdict was rendered. Young brothers with their pants drooping to their ankles and brothers with six-figure salaries and Brooks Brothers' suits saw the picture. We needed to wake up from the dream!

By the time that was over, we had a slight respite until the O. J. Simpson trial and his "not guilty" verdict. When the Simpson verdict was announced, what was the outcry of White America? "This is preposterous!" they shouted. "This is a bastardization of our judicial system." "He's gotten off scot-free!" Others literally cried. Those of us under the "illusion of inclusion" had finally awakened. For all the years that African Americans have been in the United States, we have been telling the powers-that-be there is a problem that needs to be addressed. Now they could finally see and believe that there *is* a problem.

Why couldn't they see the problem when it was Emmett Till? Where was their concern when Medgar Evers was killed, and countless others? Why weren't they upset enough to act when they saw Rodney King beaten like a runaway slave? Why didn't they fuss when the Menendez brothers got a reprieve? Why is it that, to date, we still cannot discuss the O. J. Simpson verdict in mixed company? BECAUSE THERE IS A PROBLEM!!! My world had regressed before my eyes. But what could I do? I could not change things. But what if there were at least 999,999 other individuals who felt the same urgency as I?

This March would not turn me loose!

By this time, that phrase annoyed me more than it annoys you, my reader. The fact that the call for my compliance could not be ignored was pleasantly unsettling. I now tried to excuse myself from the March on the basis of "atonement." I found myself thinking, Atonement? For what do I have to atone? I have no children that I have abandoned. I am not, nor have I ever been, abusive to any women. I work and I try to take care of my own business. So this March is not for me. But it would not turn me loose!

My cavalier attitude almost caused me to miss an opportunity to see and be a part of a march for which there could be no substitute. But God is good. I am so thankful to God for watching over babies and fools. Since I am too old to be a baby, you know under which category I fall. God finally allowed me to see clearly.

I had to atone for my selfish attitude. I had to atone for my "lip service" and lack of active participation on behalf of those who could not or would not participate. I had to atone for my indecisiveness and cynicism when someone's well-being could have been hanging in the balance. I had to be there for the brothers who felt like I felt. I had to be there!

The more I thought about it, the more vivid became my vision of a Million Man March. I could not only feel the need, but I could see the benefit for all.

By this time, I embraced the Million Man March with a restrained passion. While my father had gone on to glory, I was still blessed to be in the company of my father's brother and my cousin.

We arrived on the Mall about 9:30 A.M. Hundreds of thousands of men were already there. About 10:00 A.M., brother Dick Gregory said, "We have reached the one million mark. What that means is that at 10:00 on October 16, 1995, one million Black women knew where their [loved ones] were." This comical remark, however, in no way overshadowed the awesome power that one million united, peaceful Black men represented.

There isn't a word that can express the feeling we all felt. My father had a term that he used to explain such a feeling; he called it "Outrageous Joy." I will have to borrow his term, as it seems to be the only way I can describe what I felt on that great day.

In the days since the March, I have tried to consistently evaluate myself—not constantly, but consistently. I have found that constant evaluation is slightly masochistic but consistent is fair. I try to write something about each day or at least each week. I advise anyone who is not already keeping some type of journal to do so. We all know the value of history. It is important to keep our own. In this way, no one can distort our stories, though they may try.

In a lot of churches throughout the nation there are groups being started and activities being planned. The "One Church, One Addict" program has been replicated by churches in the Baltimore area.

African American men must get interested in such projects. They must get involved in community organizations or activities. Take a stand in the political arena. Every year I am involved with someone's campaign. Sometimes my candidate wins. Sometimes they lose. I try not to get caught up in the winning or the losing. As long as I believe in my candidate and he or she has principles that I can support, I will get involved. When I can no longer find those who can factor in that equation, perhaps it will be time for me to stand up and be heard.

I have an enlarged picture of the Million Man March stapled to my door. The picture was taken from behind the podium, and the panoramic view encompasses as many of the men as the lens could capture. Every time I leave my apartment, it reminds me of the people, the emotion, my responsibility to not only get involved but to stay involved.

I try to live by simple rules. Before I make any business or personal decisions, I try to place myself in the other person's shoes. I often ask myself, "Would I want or need to be treated like this?" I treat everyone as an individual. I strongly believe that to whom much is given, much is expected. I try to remember we are now in the days of the "Noah Principle," where there are no prizes for predicting rain, only for building arks.

I challenge African American people to get involved and stay involved. Become active in your own community in a positive fashion. Network and branch out. Some of you can help take care of our elders. Others of you can help raise our youth. Be a positive voice in spite of a negative society. Speak to someone you do not know. Go out and commit a random act of kindness every day. When you are blessed with a gut feeling that will not TURN YOU LOOSE, follow it, for it may change your outlook on life forever.

God bless and take care.

One for All and All for One

F. ALLISON PHILLIPS

"One Million Men and One God"—this was the caption on one of hundreds of signs that expressed the vision and reality of the history-making event held at the Capitol Mall on October 16, 1995. Minister Louis Farrakhan and Rev. Dr. Benjamin Chavis had issued the call for African American men to come together for "A Day of Atonement, Reconciliation, and Responsibility."

Black men across the nation heeded the call and came to Washington, D.C., by car, train, bus, and airplane, just to be a part of this spiritual event. Fathers, sons, grandfathers, uncles, brothers, and friends; Black men from all walks of life stood shoulder to shoulder, symbolizing strength and solidarity. It was truly a sight to behold and remember.

We stood on the very grounds where, on auction blocks, our ancestors were sold as slaves. We honored the spirits of our ancestors as we stood together in unity on this holy day. Black Christians and Muslims atoned for past neglect of our families and communities and took a pledge of responsibility to end violence, to honor and respect ourselves and our families, and to uplift our communities.

The passage of Scripture that defined this Day of Atonement was 2 Chronicles 7:14: "If my people who are called by my name humble themselves, pray, seek my face, and turn from their wicked ways, then I will hear from heaven, and will forgive their sin and heal their land."

Christian and Islamic prayer and praise pierced the air on Sunday night and punctuated the Monday event. A strong God presence defined who we were and what we were about. Great power and joy were experienced when a million Black men sang "Lift Every Voice and Sing."

Speaker after speaker defined our historic and contemporary realities and issued future challenges. Never before in our history in America have African American men felt so understood and affirmed. Power salutes, applause, solidarity handshakes, and embraces were the order of the day. The poetry of Maya Angelou; a speech from our mother of the civil rights movement, Rosa Parks; and words from Dorothy Height and Betty Shabazz affirmed the event and lifted the vision of brothers and sisters working together to create a better future for our people.

Perhaps the words of Stevie Wonder's song defined the future vision of peace with justice: "one for all and all for one" within the African American community and all humankind.

I shared the day with two nephews. We bonded in new ways as we shared the joy of this Million Man March. We left the March feeling that our manhood was affirmed and challenged spiritually and culturally. It was a blessing to share this day of atonement with hundreds of other United Church of Christ Black men who stood shoulder to shoulder, willing and ready to embrace the vision and one another. The words of the song sung at the end of the day were very appropriate: "To God Be the Glory!"

Imagine Our New Greatness

DOUGLAS S. LEE

In 1995, on October sixteenth, the momentous event known as the Million Man March took place. On this date, a million Black men gathered on the Mall of our nation's capital for a day of unity, love, and oneness with themselves, their brothers, and God.

African American men arrived from all across the country to be a part of this groundbreaking, historic occasion, and to hear a myriad of speakers, intellectuals, and leaders.

Among the speakers was the Minister Louis Farrakhan, leader of the Nation of Islam and one of the organizers of the Million Man March. Minister Farrakhan, who is a controversial man, was the reason why many Blacks and Whites alike denounced the March. They said they would not support or be a part of anything associated with Louis Farrakhan, because of his beliefs and the beliefs of his religion. However, at no time during Minister Farrakhan's speech did he advocate Islam as the greatest religion, ask for converts to Islam, or defile the beliefs of any other religion. This March was not about Louis Farrakhan. This March was not about the Nation of Islam. This March was about one million Black men and one unity.

During the speeches, songs, and prayers of the Million Man March, points that were long overdue were voiced, such as unity and peace in the African American community. Facts that had been hidden and buried for so long were unearthed and given to an unseeing mass of people in the hopes of opening their eyes. Facts such as: There are more Black men in prison than in college. Facts such as: African Americans, who constitute only 12 percent of this nation's population, constitute over 50 percent of the population in prison.

Songs that had not been heard for generations were sung in their native languages. Prayers were shared by the doctor, the dentist, the policeman, the politician, and the drug dealer, all of whom promised to reform their ways in this dawning of a new era for African Americans.

Much was gained from the Million Man March. There was unity on this day among a million African American men; there were strength and love, worship and peace. Also, they learned. They learned about their rich African heritage. They learned about the African goddess—the Black woman. Perhaps the most important fact they learned is that they will never, ever make it in this world without one another.

Now I must change the "*they*" into a "*we*," because I was among those Black men who gained from the Million Man March. However, I hope and feel that we will gain a great deal more from the Million Man March. I have a hope that the thirst for knowledge that was sparked at the March was not satiated. I and other African American men will want to know about our royal lineage, not just our slave lineage.

I have a hope that all the naysayers in the African American community can come together with the organizers, participants, and followers of the March to reach a common goal in the spiritual, economic, educational, and physical betterment of our people. We will prosper as a people only if *all* of our people are united. If not, we will fall as a people.

I have a hope that a universal unity between African American men will be gained. It *must* be gained. We must unite because we can no longer afford to kill one another. Reasons explaining why we kill one another have been voiced en masse; however, the true reason is lack of self-worth. A man once said "Your soul is priceless, but you'll die for free." The Million Man March assigned worth to Black men.

I have a hope that those who were at the March will go back and teach those who were not—teach them to love, honor, and respect themselves, their brothers, their women, and their God.

I have a hope that one million African American men will gain the inspiration to change. And if only one does change, the Million Man March will be well worth it. And I *know* one who has changed, for that one is *me*.

These are my hopes for the gains inspired by the Million Man March. Hopes that I feel *will* come to pass in the near future. Imagine the magnitude of the changes that will come about. Imagine our new direction. Imagine our new greatness as Black men. Imagine.

The Power of the Message

DAVID P. GARDNER

At the 1995 celebration of the Omega Psi Phi Founders Day, I shared a spiritually motivating experience with my Omega brothers. You see, we are bonded by four cardinal principles, written by our four founding fathers: manhood, scholarship, perseverance, and uplift. Inspired, ignited, and seriously influenced by the Million Man March, we appeared strengthened by number at our breakfast meeting. We were full of resolve and ready to take action!

My chapter brothers answered a call from a community organization in Harlem that cried out in a way that stirred our fathers to tears. This was and is a cause to unite and atone.

As an Omega man who attended the Million Man March, I am challenged as a Black man with a commitment to succeed. On October 16, 1995, in Washington, D.C., there on the Mall emerged a mighty message to African American men—a message that will be remembered every day in every city and community. Our challenges are steadfast, and we look forward to consciously and effectively making a difference.

I, and other men, are constantly made aware and troubled by the lack of Black men as positive role models in our communities. The Gonzaga Program of St. Aloysius School reminds me of this. St. Aloysius has a tradition of providing quality education to inner-city young and gifted men. These young men, for the most part, come from single-parent families and are without role models and without a source that binds them. Likewise, they are financially handicapped.

We, men of heritage and honor, have to complete the task our parents have started. Because of this, we are organizing a chapter follow-up to the Million Man March in the form of our commitment to the Gonzaga Program. We have organized a program that will emphasize the development of personal leadership, relationships, self-esteem, and academic achievements for middle-school young men. Our role is to be mentors, tutors, and big brothers to these students.

Through our efforts, we also have been able to give financial assistance to students and their families. The school's faculty, administration, and parents look forward to a long partnership with us. This program is an example of how the men in our chapter of Omega Psi Phi Fraternity, Inc., can promote and implement the spirit of the Million Man March.

There is a renewed sense of involvement in our endeavors as a result of the March. This enthusiasm is shown toward the program and manifests itself in projects that greatly affect the students for the better.

The message from the March is clear, resoundingly clear. Black men who are the shining pearls of civilization must come together. True power lies in numbers. Are we not immobilized by our indifferences? Are we not overwhelmed by our struggles? Can we not erase the history that embellishes the footprints of an enslaved and shackled people and come together to free our future?

We must replace dope and despair with hope and repair. Our children—the targets of torture and genocide—need our love, not homicide. If, with each waking moment, each breath taken, we must be reminded of the love and nurture from our forebears, then so be it. The power of the message is the power of the people.

Countering the Conspiracy

JAWANZA KUNJUFU

It was a day that I will never forget. No one knew how many men would be in Washington, D.C. Our excitement swelled when Benjamin Chavis told us there were a hundred thousand men assembled Sunday night!

On Monday morning, when I stepped up on the speaker's platform, I knew the major event was not on the platform but in the crowd of a million. Everyone was visibly pleased and in extreme awe. You could look in the brothers' eyes and see their enthusiasm, commitment to our race, and the peace from God which truly transcends all understanding.

On October 16, 1995, Washington, D.C., was the safest and the best place for any African American man to rest his feet.

My role as a speaker at the March was to emphasize the need to save our boys. My best-selling book, *Countering the Conspiracy to Destroy Black Boys,* gave me full ammunition. I shared with over a million brothers that we could save our men if we taught them as boys how to read, write, compute, and become computer literate.

Incarceration did not begin in prison. It began near fourth grade, when our boys' test scores declined and they were placed in special education classes—suspended, expelled, and literally "pushed out" of schools.

I implored our men to become active with our boys, because 70 percent of them live without fathers in the home; have never experienced a male teacher; or have never seen any man read a book, write a letter, operate a computer, or pray to God.

The speeches began at 6:30 A.M. Minister Farrakhan concluded the March at about 6:30 P.M. Over a million men stood and listened attentively for over twelve hours. I agreed with the March for symbolic and solidarity purposes, but I knew the effectiveness of the March would be in the days to come.

Where do we go from here? What do we do now? First, there was very little atonement that transpired on that great day. Many of us have not reconciled with each other. There were many men on the platform and in the crowd who have been abusive and negligent with their spouses and other love ones.

The first order of business is that we must reconcile family issues. Second, we must reconcile any issues with members in the liberation struggle. Third, we must all join an organization and contribute our money and volunteer a minimum of two hours weekly. Fourth, we must develop more after-school and Saturday cultural-awareness academies, tutorial and test-taking centers, Rites of Passage programs, mentoring programs, Junior Business Leagues, and crime-watch groups.

Lastly, we must surrender our all to God. As men, we no longer can believe that placing God first in our lives is a sign of weakness. We can't assume our position as head of the house until God is head of our lives.

The Trumpet Sounds

PAUL S. BURLEY

Beneath the loud trumpet call of the Million Man March was the sound of a steady drumbeat, a sound that urges each Black man and woman to do his or her own part to uplift the race. On October 16, 1995, we all got stirred up together. Each of our rhythms filled our collective conscience, and we needed an outlet—fast. In 1992, some of it was released on the streets of Los Angeles. In Washington, D.C., we ignited our fuel again. We erupted over that same goal, justice. But, this time, we used a different means to address it. This time we had a big plan.

Any victory from this trumpet call would be manifested by what would be brought back to, and come up with at, our local bargaining tables. As a people, we already know that we have to "unify, unify, unify!" We know we've got to "keep hope alive." Still, all those platitudes have gone unheard. Before we can see the forest, we have to plant the trees!

The more precise question is not "What now?," but rather "What *thing* do we now *do?*" For each of us, that should mean making at least one change in our daily routine. The majority of us will find this change right outside our own front door; it's what we pass when we go out and come in. I'm talking about the opportunities we overlook when we neglect to support Black-owned businesses.

Day in and day out these merchants and professionals open their doors to us. And every day, in many cases, we pass them by, only to give our money to the ones who do not have our best interests at heart. And often, when we think that these people cheerfully enjoy the competitive edge we give them, they assume that the Black men who entered their business have come to steal, rather than to buy.

Last winter, a middle-aged African American couple were strip-searched in Victoria's Secret under suspicion of stealing undergarments. It was later found that no crime had been committed. However, it was reported that the couple had their most intimate body parts searched for missing merchandise. How unnecessary! How disgraceful! Now that Victoria's "secret" is out, should our women buy from this store?

If only a *portion* of those in attendance at the March—let's say 250,000—made the commitment to spend their money in a store owned by a Black businessperson, Black businesses would be far more financially stable by the first anniversary of the March. Today, for example, we could have more services and better products displayed on the shelves of the neighborhood grocery. The nearby computer dealer could have moved from a basement space to a storefront on the avenue. One of the too-few Black-owned bookstores might have opened a new location near you. The local jeweler may have finally set up her shop on the boulevard so that she could stop having to rent booths at small trade shows. Quality merchandise would have come "uptown" if demand were uptown.

This year, while eating carry-out chicken, who said, "We can't market this product"? And who said, "Black folks can't make pizza"?

Let me tell you the story of the African farmer. One day a farmer sold his big farm for less than half what it was worth so that he could search for riches. He traveled far and wide, but he found no wealth. Discouraged, the farmer finally gave up and threw himself into a river.

One day, the man to whom the farmer sold his land was walking along a stream in the middle of the farm. He looked down and saw a shining stone in the water. He reached down and pulled it out. He couldn't make anything of it, so he took it home and put it on his mantle, as a conversation piece. Some months later, a houseguest remarked what a beautiful stone it was. The owner simply said he found it in the stream that ran through the middle of the farm. In fact, he said there were hundreds just like it, maybe even thousands.

After taking a closer look, the houseguest asked the owner if he knew what he'd stumbled upon. To the owner's surprise, the houseguest told him he had found a diamond! The two men became partners, and each spent the rest of his days very wealthy.

I think you understand the moral of this story: We can support our own best interests by supporting our own businesses. For many of us, they're easier to get to, because they are in our community. Whatever they need to improve upon can be accomplished in part by more support. We will understand that *we* made all this possible.

What next? Will we begin building responsible schools? Will we dare buy up television stations or start new dimensions of media? Will we make these ventures possible by establishing new banks and making collective money decisions?

If we support our businesses, this year's actions will speak volumes. And this foundation could be the rock upon which we build a magnificent empire.

It does not appear to be difficult to understand, nor should it. Nor do the rhythms or the pulse that emanate after the trumpet has sounded.

A Sweet Spirit

HOWARD BROOKINS SR.

The Million Man March was a day that I will always remember. Our day began at Midway Airport. My son, Howard Jr., and I flew to Washington, D.C., with a group of fathers, sons, and other concerned men from Trinity United Church of Christ. We were in a group of about twenty-five to thirty Black males. We, of course, drew much attention.

Upon our arrival in Washington, D.C., we had prayer and thanked God for a safe passage. We took the Metro system to the Mall. There were so many people—so many that we lost sight of our group! It was truly something to see! It was impossible to stay together. We watched the speakers on monitors since we were about three football-field lengths from the stage.

We saw Masons. We saw fraternity brothers. My son saw members of his fraternity. We even saw people from Chicago with whom we had not come. It was just an overwhelming situation.

The spirit was even more overwhelming. There was a sweet spirit permeating the air. The spirit was powerful. The respect, unity, and love were evident everywhere. People didn't even smoke. The spirit of peace was so strong that if you bumped into someone, that person would apologize for you!

In the African American community, one of the biggest faux pas is to step on another person's shoes. There was none of that, even though we were elbow to elbow. A powerful divine spirit took over the crowd. It moved from man to man to man. It was indeed a blessing.

The Million Man March has moved people to change. I have seen a change in the men who attended the March, and I have seen a change in my own life.

I enjoyed all of the speeches; however, there was an important message that I got out of Farrakhan's speech. He emphasized the importance of joining an organization. Through organized efforts, a person can exhibit strength that he or she does not have as an individual, be it religious, political, or otherwise. For example, we know that a person can praise God at home and elsewhere. However when one joins a church and becomes a part of the body of Christ, it reinforces one's effort and gives one the strength to continue.

Likewise, through a political body, one can vote as an individual. However, if a person belongs to a political group, that person can do much more. Therefore, it is important to be involved in something *with* someone. This is, to me, one of the most powerful things Farrakhan stated.

One of the greatest feelings I felt was when I stood next to my son among a million African American men. We had the opportunity to reflect over our lives and over our relationship with each other. This was the high point of the entire day.

Upon my return home, I had the opportunity to have an in-depth conversation with him concerning why we attended the March. The opportunity I had to be with him, to stand shoulder to shoulder, man to man, was enlightening and gratifying.

I looked at him and realized how fast children grow. If, at any time, you can spend quality time with your children, do it. As African American people, it is often difficult to spend quality time with our children because of our efforts to survive. The March made me reflect on the things I have done with my son throughout his life.

What must we do now? I believe more African Americans must become entrepreneurs. As a businessman, the hours are long and the pay might be small, but it is well worth it because you are your own person. You have a pride that others don't have. You also have a sense of accomplishment. We, as African American people, make the mistake of sending our children to college to get an education so that they can get a good job working for someone else. We should strive to send our children to college so that they can use their talents and intelligence to work for themselves and in their communities as entrepreneurs.

I certainly will remember attending the Million Man March. It has changed my life forever.

The Goal Was Accomplished

HOWARD B. BROOKINS JR.

October 16, 1995, began with great hope and expectation for what was to be billed as the largest gathering of African American men. For me, the day started with an early-morning trip to the airport, where men from my church met to take a flight to Washington, D.C. I arrived at the airport anxious and optimistic as to what to expect. There was a great sense of excitement and exhilaration at the airport. Fathers, sons, and grandparents posed for pictures. Men greeted other men with hugs.

As we waited for our flight to depart, we gathered around radios and televisions to hear about the estimated attendance. There were immediate cheers when the estimates returned larger than those projected by the media. Before it was time to board the plane, we all gathered in a circle and prayed for safe passage. The passersby seemed to stare in disbelief. They seemed to be astonished by our numbers and resolve.

This sentiment seemed to be echoed by the majority media. They trotted out expert scientists and mathematicians to tell the general public that it would be improbable or impossible for the promoters to attain their goal. The major newspapers, as well as local and national networks, could not help but put their spin on what they believed the message should be and why the message should be dismissed because of the messenger.

Reporters interviewed prominent African American men and requested that they denounce the promoter and the March. They looked for hidden meanings in the idea. They said that to support the March would somehow validate all of the views of its promoter. They interviewed prominent African American women to request that they denounce the March for their exclusion. However, the controversial sponsor was soon to be overshadowed by the symbolic meaning of the event.

While I sat in the Chicago airport waiting for our flight to depart, I could not have predicted the profound impact this event would have on my life and the life of every African American man in this country. Upon arrival at the airport in Washington, D.C., and throughout the day, I observed men shaking hands, embracing, and showing a sense of jubilation. It was overwhelming to see more than a million African American men standing in unison for a positive cause and in a peaceful demonstration.

The March had accomplished its goal. On October 16, 1995, the world looked at Washington, D.C., and saw that African American men could stand for something positive and ask for nothing in return. Since the March, we have affirmed that a million African American men can stand together in unity—from all walks of life and socioeconomic backgrounds—without one incident of violence.

We have already given our communities a sense of pride, dignity, and respect. We have already made our communities stronger just by being active. We have strengthened our stand in the world by showing it our resolve and our resourcefulness.

We must not forget October sixteenth. The March was a symbol of hope, and because of this, we must teach our youth that we can persevere in the face of adversity. One cannot judge its success by external barometers, but only by one's own set of values. The March was a religious experience, in that it meant many things to many people. Therefore, we should celebrate the March in different ways. However, to expect a revelation in our communities because of the March would be to set ourselves up to fail. This would only add fuel for cynics.

The March affected and motivated people in different ways. We must reflect and meditate on this experience to guide our lives toward what is best for us as individuals, which will, in turn, be best for our communities. We must become the revelation.

Umoja!

LAWRENCE OLIVER HALL

My fifteen-year-old son and I left Canaan Baptist Church at 5 A.M. along with about ninety-six other brothers from my church. The three-hour bus ride on Interstate 95 was full of anticipation and excitement. When we arrived at Robert F. Kennedy Stadium, we were surrounded by buses from all over the country.

As we began the walk to the Capitol, I was overwhelmed with the feeling of *umoja*, unity, in the air. A sea of African American men moving in the same direction with the same goal was a sight to behold. I could feel the presence of the Holy Spirit immediately.

Upon reaching the Capitol, we met even more men; more brothers than I have ever seen in my life; more than I had dreamed would attend the March. Men from all walks of life—old men, young men, boys, physically challenged men, and men of all religious backgrounds were represented. The thought that kept popping into my mind was *"God is so good!"*

It was about this time that my son and I lost sight of each other. There were just so many people. It was hard to search for him. My faith was truly tested. On one hand, as a father I was concerned for my son's safety and well-being, but I knew in my heart that he was going to be all right. My son would be fine in the hands of God and in the company of brothers committed to spiritual renewal and atonement. Everyone was so friendly. No pushing. No cursing. And, oddly enough, I saw no smoking. I did not see my son for the rest of the day, but I knew that I would see him when the time was right.

Each speaker was very moving and spirit-led, but the young man who spoke, Allendye Baptiste, brought tears to my eyes. This young boy represented the hope, strength, and genius of our youth. The singing was beautiful and healing for me. God has a way of touching the soul with a song in a special way. The brothers who were former gang leaders touched me also because I felt a real sense of peace and purpose in their message. Black-on-Black crime is an ugly disease, and the March was just what Doctor Jesus had ordered.

I took time to thank God for my life, my family, and also to ask for forgiveness for all the things that I had not done. When I have talks with God, it is in the quiet of my home or car, but to talk to God among millions is a wonderful experience.

As I began to walk back to the bus, I saw my son walking toward me. He was smiling from ear to ear. I have never been so glad to see that boy! We started talking, not about losing each other in the crowd, but about our experiences and how wonderful the March had been.

My son said that he felt safe and protected by all those brothers. He and I had planned to attend the March to strengthen our relationship and to share the experience together, but God had another plan for us. We understood and accepted it.

We listened to Minister Farrakhan's speech on the bus. If I had not known better, I would have thought I was listening to a Baptist preacher. We all said the Million Man Pledge on the bus with pride, hope, and purpose. The ride home was a time of sharing reflections, experiences, and love. Many brothers talked about how we could bring the spirit of the Million Man March back to other brothers in the community. It was then that I knew that I had to follow through with my plans to start a Rites of Passage program for the boys in my church.

The face of Allendye Baptiste kept appearing in my mind along with the fact that my son had been protected while we were separated. I had to share my time, faith, and talents with young men.

We are now moving ahead with the Canaan Male Rites of Passage Program. I see the growth in the boys already. We have the makings of a wonderful program that can help to shape the lives of young men, although, as with any new program, there is room for improvement. I know that this is what God wants me to do, and I'm so glad that I was one in a million on October 16, 1995.

Guidance from My Sisters

CARL K. HARMON

"Wow!!!" is the first thought that comes to mind when I think of the events that led up to my attending the Million Man March on October 16, 1995.

In the beginning of my journey, there were many doubters who felt it was a waste of time to attend an event given by the Nation of Islam's leader, Minister Louis Farrakhan. Many African American church leaders felt this event fueled additional hate and separation between our European counterparts and the Black community. It would be something if they knew the spiritual energy generated at this event and how it could change Black history in America!

I had little difficulty in finding African American men who wanted to gain additional fortitude by having open dialogue on the importance of this event and its direct relationship to improving our communities. Something concerned me in the beginning regarding the March: It had to do with the theme and how I perceive it. When I think of the word "atonement" and how it was used to set the atmosphere for the March, l started to wonder, "Is this another situation where Black men haven't taken responsibility for their actions, and again are being blamed for all the failures that we daily see and hear in the media?"

There are many strong and good African American men who continue to be accountable for their actions. However, for some reason, these men are never recognized for their accomplishments. I felt insulted by this theme. Initially, I had decided not to attend the event. This prompted me to have a dialogue with some African American sisters.

In our conversations, I was able to see the importance of going to the March. I learned that Black women believed there was a need for our men to come together. There was also a need to keep the key ingredient of our future as a race of people alive—that being the survival of the strong Black family. *Thank You my Beautiful Black Women for being the foundation of my strength. I will always love you.*

"Captivated" is what I felt as I stood on the lawn of the Capitol building. I was engulfed in prayer and in vision with the souls of a million men who just happened to be of African descent. I laughed, cried, and shared the disappointment of men who only want a history that they can plant and nurture throughout their existence. As I walked through the crowd, I could feel the love and togetherness among my brothers. I wished this could expand into our neighborhoods after the March.

One of the most touching moments for me was to observe an older gentleman. He was at least eighty years old. He was dressed in a beautiful African garment and carried a wooden cane. I watched as a tear ran down his face. l know this March brought back many memories for him. I only wish I could live long enough to see the future of my younger brothers and sisters.

As Minister Louis Farrakhan spoke, I could sense a bonding of brotherhood, and I understood the many challenges that lay ahead of our people. People were standing. People had climbed onto the top of streetlights and trees, and they were sitting on the steps of the Capitol building. What a beautiful sight of unity and positive images for our children and the world to see! *Yes, we, as African American men, can get along if we are given the same playing field on which to play.*

Reflecting on the events after the March, the major question that still must be answered is, "What do we do now?" How do we take the energy generated at the Million Man March and share it with our community leaders?

I think the first question for all Black men to ask themselves is, "What am I doing to make a difference in my life and in the lives of those who love me?" We can't help anyone until we get our own house in order. We need to understand that we can't help everybody, but we certainly can help somebody. We can influence others, especially our children, by making our dreams reality and showing a loving spirit.

So, Black men of the world, take your faces out of the palms of your hands and stand tall. Be leaders. Challenge the conditions in your communities. Get involved in community and economic development and set a path for others to follow. Take the initiative to say how you want to live, and do not allow the perils of society to dictate your lives. Only then can we make a different in our lives as well as in the lives of our families.

Peace, my brothers.

The Long Arm of History

AUSTIN J. DUNN JR.

I did not want to go.

"Why?" I asked myself. "Why do I need to go to Washington, D.C., to attend the Million Man March?" The March was billed as a Day of Atonement and Reconciliation. Why did I have to atone? Reconciliation, for what?

The long arm of history touched my soul. I changed my mind. The Middle Passage, slavery, Jim Crow, the civil rights movement—all are a part of the glorious and painful history of the African American presence in this great nation. To rouse and stir, to last and prevail, this American history, this struggle, demanded that the Million Man March take place.

The excitement and camaraderie on the bus ride to Washington, D.C., were almost overwhelming. A spiritual blanket of snow seemed to cover the riders from head to toe. I asked many marchers why they came. Almost to a person, the responses were that it felt right to be there. Were the speakers important? No. Was Louis Farrakhan important? No. What mattered was that over a million African American men came to the nation's capital—a symbol of the greatest nation on earth—and stood as yet another symbol, of the best of manhood, responsibility, courage, triumph, spirit, and soul.

Where do African Americans go now? We keep going to the places we have always gone. We must keep going to God. We must keep going to our parents. We must keep going to our children. The love from God, guidance from our parents, and nurturing of our children will give meaning to our lives. It always has, and it will be right.

Ralph Waldo Emerson once said, "To be simple is to be great." There are simple things we can do in our own lives that will continue the struggle to expand our democracy. Every African American eighteen years old or older can vote. Every African American can share his or her talent or skill with one person. Every African American can practice loving one child. Every African American can save ten cents of every dollar he or she earns. Simple deeds. One deed. Great deeds. Practicing freedom, practicing responsibility, practicing love. These are timeless deeds that we can do to make freedom real, make democracy come·alive, and make our lives meaningful.

Simple, but great.

Called by God

MORRIS ALLEN JR.

The Million Man March was an awe-inspiring event. It was an event that I certainly will never, ever forget, and it's one of those situations where you had to be there in order to experience its depth. There was just an aura in the air.

This March was unlike any event I have ever witnessed. The exhilaration of seeing your favorite team win a championship was of no comparison. It was an event that I honestly believe had been called by God.

Everyone who attended was there for a purpose—that of atonement and reconciliation. I stood among a million Black men who were strong and unified. They came to Washington, D.C., with the desire to effect a social change in their community as well as to find personal things that they could do with their lives. In my estimation, we should have done this a long time ago.

I was especially pleased and proud to have my son with me. I know that he will never forget this event, and he will never, ever forget seeing all of those men assembled.

Personally, I believe that this March allowed my son to gain an inner strength that he did not have before. He was able to see that Black men are strong; we are men of God. And he learned that he can do anything that he wants to do if he has the power of the Holy Spirit behind him.

The purposes that moved men to attend the March—atonement and reconciliation—were actions that I already had subscribed to in my life. Nevertheless, the March solidified what I already espoused in my life and what I already stood for.

The March helped many men to make a conscious effort to do the right thing in the future. Additionally, this event made me more conscious of what I did around my home, with my family, and in my community.

In terms of what we could do with youth, we can begin programs similar to what we have at my church, Trinity United Church of Christ. We have formed a "Million for the Master" ministry. This ministry brings together men and women from various backgrounds to help youth become more familiar with their roots. The young people can also be assisted in many ways by adults who have access to many other people who can also help. By doing this, I think we will be able to better educate our children to let them know that we have to unite in order for everyone to grow.

I honestly and genuinely believe that, if nothing else, the March made brothers aware of their presence in this country. We recognized that we are truly God's creation. And, as such, we have to stand up and be proud that we are God's creation, irrespective of our color.

I also honestly believe that brothers are much more sincere in their attempts to have relationships with their women and with their children. I also think that the March has made brothers stand up and be strong Black men in the name of God.

Now that the March is over, I would hope that African American men will first become spiritual men. Second, I hope we will become focused on our economic power. Third, I think that once we gain and understand our economic power, we will create opportunities for others so that we can build our own economic base and future.

Thousands upon Thousands

DAVID B. MILLER

The Million Man March, for me, was an opportunity to join with my brothers in a collective opportunity for atonement. As many of our communities slide into disrepair and others peer at the abyss of naked hedonism and self-indulgence, the March provided a new direction, a new challenge for our own destiny. A destiny defined by us and us only. A destiny that will enable us to return to our communities with a collective sense of self-respect and love. As African American men, the March's call for atonement made those of us who were present and those who were not, reexamine our contributions to our problems and also consider how we could and should be active contributors in the solution.

While many around the country expressed trepidation that the March would establish Minister Louis Farrakhan as the leader for all of Black America, I, as well as my colleagues, knew that this old practice was fear disguised as concern. I knew that, for decades, many of the leaders for, and in, Black America have been anointed by those outside of our communities in order to maintain control over us. However, this March was about us, African Americans, defining who should and could speak for our communities. The amazing awareness that the March made clearer was that all of us can and should speak to the problems in our community.

This collective gathering of African American men showed to the nation and the world that we can and will be heard in arenas that are not defined by the boundaries of an athletic field or the razor wire of a correctional facility. We defined ourselves as men, husbands, fathers, brothers, protectors, and supporters of our own.

From the time I arrived at the airport, the anticipation for the March was running high. I remember a woman who held a sign welcoming all the brothers to the March. Not only did she look like my mother-in-law, but she introduced me to a brother from Iowa.

After a few minutes of conversation with this brother, I found out that he knew my best friend from my childhood days in North Carolina. True to his word, when he returned home, he told my friend that he had met me. My friend called soon afterwards. We have remained in touch since that time.

I remember the brothers at the hotel and the positive greetings extended at each corner. There were no colors or signs, just "What's happening?" or "Where you from?" or "Ain't this beautiful!"

I remember the brother who was the chef at a hotel making sure that everyone had enough to eat before heading out to the March. I recall the sight of the hundreds of thousands of proud African American men of all ages on the trains and buses headed to the Capitol grounds. Minister Farrakhan's call for us to "come sober and tall" was clearly evident as my companions and I boarded the train.

The initial sight of all of my brothers and some sisters was truly a beautiful experience. Everywhere you looked, there we were. Talking, respecting, greeting, and, more importantly, showing the world that we could gather peacefully. For me, the most moving moment was not the speeches but the call to sing "Lift Every Voice and Sing." The sound of a million proud Black voices will forever be etched into my memory. Given America's negative stereotypes of us, I am sure that many Americans who viewed this historic event had to deal with a significant level of cognitive dissonance. The violent and decadent behavior that many had hoped and predicted would occur, did not.

Since returning from the March, I have made it my point to speak and meet my brothers with a positive greeting. My companions and I organized several post-March discussions since the March. We did this so that we could continue a dialogue of the strategies started at the March. I also became involved in the men's group at my church in order to continue the growth that I experienced through the March.

Our Wounds Are Deep

LARRY GRANT COLEMAN

The Million Man March was unlike anything I have ever experienced. It was something that I imagined my spirit and heart wanted to happen for African American men and the larger African American community. As a result of our being raped, murdered, and stolen from our African ancestral home, the experience of the Million Man March represented an important part of healing for our people.

I recently traveled to Ghana, West Africa, and visited two of the castles where many of our ancestors were held before being shipped to the Americas. During the visit to these enslavement locations, we experienced a ritual reenactment of the capture and transportation of the Africans.

We walked through the holding cells and through the "gate of no return." We stood outside and reflected momentarily. We then returned inside to a renewing or "coming home" celebration of drummers and dancers. We all needed to know, firsthand, about the tragedy of our ancestors' enslavement to help us reckon with the difficulty of our being descendants of African captives living in America.

Our wounds are deep, and we carry them with us everywhere we go. However, we need powerful, ritualistic, cultural experiences to more effectively clarify our own identities and those of our families.

The March was another such healing experience that African American men needed in order to go on with their lives, to clarify their identities, to begin healing family wounds, and to begin to think about how to leave a positive legacy for succeeding generations. I believe that most of the men who attended were changed for the better and cannot help but have a changed agenda for their lives.

Clearly one of the new agenda items for African Americans is to heal our families and communities *ourselves*. Our children and our families must be our priorities, not our selfish desires. To this end,

I underscore the suggestion by Dr. Jawanza Kunjufu that we all become involved in the lives of our children and other people's children (those who may not have the support they need) in order to help those children become successful, focused, spiritually developed individuals.

This has already been translated into one midwestern brother's idea of a "National African American Parent Involvement Day." On this day, parents, uncles, aunts, brothers, cousins, and interested "together" adults can visit their children's schools and teachers. They could also spend the entire day in support of their children's education and discipline.

I would further suggest that this idea become expanded in every community to an annual "Involvement Week" or an annual "Involvement Month." *Our children are dying in front of our eyes, and their dreams of living and creating are being destroyed in homes and classrooms every day. We must intervene in whatever way we can to help them and support their growth and development. Black women and men must get involved with our own and with other people's children.*

I would encourage us to lift up our wives, partners, children, students, clergy, supervisors, and other workers "who do something good" and acknowledge that they are quite capable of doing many good things.

As a professional storyteller and educator, I would also strongly encourage our people to celebrate our rich African oral tradition. By learning and using African folktales and proverbs, we can teach our children about their identity and about important values.

Each adult should make a commitment to tell a story that has a positive message to another adult or to a child within their community. This should be done each week of every year. Each of us should share an African and a biblical proverb with our children and one another daily. We can learn these stories and proverbs from library books, from the Bible, and from other people, particularly those who are elders within our communities.

Finally, we also can include stories and lessons of positive personal experiences in our regular sharing. There is power in our words and in our oral tradition. Proverbs 18:21 says, "Death and life are in the power of the tongue."

A Little Brother's Request

LARRY GRANT COLEMAN

(for Nathaniel Allen and little Nick Coleman)

Hey Daddy! Can I go to that march
with you
and a million men?
I'll keep in step with everyone
I promise,
even if I have to run
every now and then.

Daddy!
Is this gonna be a parade
with marching boys and girls
with tumblers and a majorette
making flips and twists and twirls?

Will there be a great big marching band
with a big horn and a drummer?
Like the one we saw in Tallahassee
when we were there last summer.

Daddy! Can I march with you
and a million men?
I'll keep up with everyone
even if I have to run
every now and then.

Oh! I see. It's not that kind of thing;
a "re-vival" for our race? . . .
But do you think they'll let me march
if I promise to keep up the pace?

I hear them talking about the march on T.V.
every day,

it's mostly negative
about that man
the stuff I hear them say.

Daddy I agree with you
it's really for "the men to heal,"
it's a "supremely special" day.
If they say something mean about it
I won't believe a word they say.

There are many people son
who seem helpless and unwise,
they sit around on their behinds
and with very undeveloped minds
they do nothing more than criticize,
nothing more than criticize.

But can I go to that march
with you and a million men.
I promise to keep up
with everyone
even if I have to run
every now and then.

This event is sacred son
and it is healing for the race
because the things we'll commit together for
have been difficult to face.

Men like your dad are going there
to clean deep wounds and heal scarred lives
to apologize to the people we've hurt
sons, daughters, fathers, mothers,
our sisters and our wives.
This gathering will help us to start
healing old deep wounds
becoming better and better men;
promising before each other
"never again, never again."

Those of us who are hurting
have caused others a lot of pain;
but we'll stand up at that Million Man March
to say "never again, never again."

I pray that when we gather there, son
with blessings from above
we'll mobilize our strength
and celebrate our love.

Yeah! You can come to that march
with me,
and a million men.
And if we do have to *run*
to keep in step with everyone,
I'll pick you up and I'll carry you
every now and then,
every now and then.

An Astounding Assignment

BEN HOLBERT

My career often affords me the opportunity to observe milestones of national and historic significance. I went to Detroit with a group of college students in 1990 when Nelson Mandela made his United States tour, appearing at Tiger Stadium. I hit the campaign trail when Arkansas Governor Bill Clinton swept through Weirton, West Virginia, on his celebrated bus tour to the White House. I even traveled to Cape Canaveral to watch the July 1995 launch of the space shuttle *Discovery*.

These were all extraordinary events. However, none made more of a personal impact on my life, or gave me a greater feeling of anticipation, than my October 16, 1995, assignment. I work as a television news reporter for the CBS affiliate in Cleveland. I was among a platoon of journalists deployed to Washington, D.C., to cover the Million Man March.

My crew and I arrived Sunday, the day before the March. I was intoxicated by the peace and unity clearly evident on the Capitol Mall. Hundreds of people had already assembled. Husbands were with their wives. Fathers were with their sons. They were walking and talking and embracing total strangers. It bore a striking resemblance to a family reunion. I often struggled with my own impulses to put down the microphone and bond with others who share our common ancestry.

What happened was absolutely astounding! Black men from Cleveland to the Caribbean, from Lexington to London, joined for a common purpose. The hairs on the back of my neck raised as I pondered how this historic event might inspire leadership, renew vision, encourage political action and personal responsibility.

Among the largest rallies ever assembled, the Million Man March filled the Capitol Mall to overflowing. It was a massive display of boys to men, babies to seniors, and Christians to Muslims. The CBS news bureau was perched high atop the federal labor building. Our TV cameras could pan the enormous corridor, from the Capitol steps to the Washington Monument. I was shocked when the National Park Service announced the attendance figure. From my vantage point, it was closer to a million than the four hundred thousand the Service had suggested.

In order for the March to achieve a modicum of success, the turnout would have to take a back seat to individual commitment. Returning home to work on and solve the problems plaguing our communities would now be the measure of success.

While on this assignment, I interviewed many people. I was particularly touched by the words of a young woman from Arlington, Virginia, who had attended the March despite the fact that organizers had asked women to stay home. She said, "I prayed that they left their guns, knives, and other weapons of human destruction at home."

Fortunately, history will record that no incidents of violence occurred during the Million Man March. (The only fatality that day involved a sixty-nine-year-old man from South Carolina who died of a heart attack. According to his family, he was overstimulated by the massive display of unity.)

She went on to tell me that rarely had she ever received "voluntary" respect from Black men. Peering into the camera, she spoke of how they had approached her at the March, in pleasant, nonthreatening terms: "Hello, sister," "Good morning," "Excuse me, sister," as they made their way past her that day. "That's how they talked to me," she said. "They were acting like real gentlemen." She added, "It made me feel like a queen!" I replied, "Isn't that the way it's supposed to be?" We smiled. We both knew the answer was yes.

As you read this book of reflections, remember the Almighty has entrusted men to protect women. The Million Man March should give pause, to ensure that African American men *first* respect themselves; then respect can be given to others much more easily. Present a positive attitude, and the benefits will be worth millions to us and to our community, now and forever!

The Clarion Call

WARDELL J. PAYNE

Examine yourselves, and only then eat of the bread and drink of the cup.

—1 Corinthians 11:28

There was definitely a divine order in the schedule of events on October 16, 1995. Surely God had ordained it! What an awesome sight it was to see Black men coming together to pray; to reflect on their duties and responsibilities as men, husbands, brothers, and keepers of the community; and to hear a message relating to our next step as a part of becoming what God intends for us to be as a people.

It was definitely a special day for me, my son, brother-in-law, father-in-law, pastor, and fellow male parishioners. We assembled early at our church for prayer, praise, and instructions. Some of our sisters in the faith were there, too. They desired to demonstrate, once again, that they wanted us to be all that we could be and that they were proud of our willingness to take a stand. They, too, were aware that the call for collective action was controversial and challenging to us.

As Christian men, we were somewhat perplexed. We understood the clarion call for unity. We were supportive of the idea, yet we were also cautious to endorse a brother whose agenda was questionable and whose theology was definitely not supported by our own religious views.

Many critics charged that we were "sleeping with the enemy." We came to determine for ourselves just what the message of the day would be. We did not endorse. We listened and visibly demonstrated that although we are diverse people of color, we still are capable of responding in unity. We, too, are sick and tired of seeing our people, our sons and daughters, our brothers and sisters, our mothers and fathers, and our friends and acquaintances, disrespected and unfairly treated.

Our assemblage did not mean that we did not appreciate what had been accomplished in the history of Blacks in America. Rather, we gathered that day in sacred commemoration of the sacrifices of our forebears, and in a deep sense of realization that we must take a stand to save our children and to preserve our heritage. We did not agree with everything that was said or done. But we heard the cry of our children! We heard the plea of our women!

Fundamentally we were comforted with the spiritual understanding that we are not alone. Our frustrations are shared! We can become more than what we have been.

The irony of the day was that we were in a revival meeting, called and organized by a non-Christian who understood Christian doctrine and its mission. Minister Farrakhan's delivery was long and sometimes too mystical for most, but his message was clear. We need to atone for our failure to be the stabilizing influence that God ordained us to be. We need not make excuses. We only need to look deep within our hearts and act responsibly. If we searched our hearts, we would not let the forces that attempt to divide us as a people keep us from realizing that we are one another's harvest, and that our enemy is neither Black nor White. Rather it is our own internalization of a sense of helplessness and personal despair which we must confront.

We must free our minds from the visages of slavery and servitude. We must realign ourselves with the spiritual force that has shaped and guided our destiny. We must put ourselves in the hands of the Almighty. The message was clear: We must return home and get busy healing and reclaiming the blessings that we have taken for granted—our women, our communities, our leaders, and our institutions.

We could not argue with the basic tenets of the message. Through God's divine providence, no one but us is going to save us from our problems. We have much to do, and we need to start by renewing our relationship with God and our families. We must rekindle respect, self-reliance, and cooperation.

In a personal sense, I initially felt that I should not attend the March. As a people, we have marched before, and nothing has ever come out of it. Did we expect this to be a Jericho moment, where walls would come tumbling down? Did we expect miraculous male bonding to be effected in the Black community as a result of this one event? What could we realistically expect to accomplish by a mere march, especially one that tries to get Christian men to follow a non-Christian leader?

I was really reluctant to participate until I reflected on the ministry of the late Reverend Dr. Martin Luther King Jr. Through the civil rights movement, Dr. King, a Christian leader, was able to coalesce persons of non-Christian belief in his effort to confront the social ills facing the American society. Although I was not highly involved in the movement, I remembered his difficulty in getting many of his own fellow Christians to support his work. Surely, if we are to confront today's social and economic issues, we can not allow unimportant divergences to cloud our judgment or participation.

There really would not have been an advancement in civil rights if we, as a people, had focused on the things that separated or distinguished us. The Million Man March, in a similar manner, made this message clear for me.

We could elect to remain detached and uninvolved, or we could make the choice to not blame others for our plight and become a part of the solution. Like Jesus, who saw the ills of humankind, we too can take a stand to be a vehicle for liberation, rather than be like those who sat back and criticized Dr. King, Malcolm X, Gandhi, and others for trying to address and improve the ills of their society. We remain neutral until we too are engulfed in the downward spiral that produced the denigration of humanity.

Today we stand at a spiritual crossroads. We are capable of appreciating a better lifestyle and the freedom that it has produced, but we are also aware of our responsibility to preserve and protect a legacy of hope for future generations. As we see the accomplishments for which our people have sacrificed quickly erode away by negative social forces and immature personal choices, we must not take the easy way out and withdraw from our own brothers and sisters.

We must examine ourselves as Black men, and as leaders of our race, families, communities, and social institutions. We can no longer afford to hide ourselves in the dark. We must be a light, and we must shine bright.

One in a Million

JAMES RAYMOND REID

When I first heard of the Million Man March, I didn't know what to expect, but I knew I wanted to be a part of this experience. I reflected on past marches and felt an uncertainty of where I fit in "as a Black man in America." Before leaving Cleveland, our group had a pep rally and prayer together. Although some of us were still unsure of what lay ahead, I believe we left with a feeling of unity.

The trip to Washington, D.C., was long, but the enthusiasm was high, which helped to break the monotony of the bus ride. As we arrived in Washington, the air was filled with excitement. We could see buses and cars filling the downtown streets in countless numbers.

As we arrived, our bus was briefly detained by national guard troops. Troops encouraged all members to stay on the bus and unload at Robert F. Kennedy Stadium, which was about a mile and a half from the site. There was some dissension among our group when we were forced to go to the stadium. We were right at the sight of the rally, and we saw other buses unloading. Our bus captain decided that it was best to go to the stadium, so we did.

Once we arrived at the stadium parking area, we were informed of the fare for the train and where we could get off. I, along with a group of others, decided that this was contrary to what the March had professed, which was to not support any financial institution for that day. We decided to walk as a group to avoid the long lines of thousands of people who were taking public transportation.

All disillusionments were forgotten as we approached the March site just before sunrise. It seemed as though our group of seven had bonded and that we would remain this way for the remainder of the day. The prayer at sunrise worship service was spectacular and set the tone for the day.

I joined my brothers in prayers for peace, unity, and atonement for past misfortunes, and for the speakers to deliver an effective message that would enlighten all men. Through a translator, we enjoyed prayers prayed in a native African language, music, and dance performers. This experience enhanced the spirit of the event and also set the tone for the rest of the day.

After the sun came up, the weather was perfect. Our group moved around the Mall in an attempt to get a better view. I was in awe to see so many brothers coming together with one accord. There were thousands in front of me, in back of me, to the left, and to the right. Young, old, middle-aged. Children were there. I thought to myself that this was truly a blessing from God to experience this historic event. As we waited for the speakers, our group walked around and enjoyed the many cultural foods and crafts displayed. We also had the opportunity to share personal experiences with each other.

When the first speaker came on, the mood of the crowd became subdued and serious. Each speaker had a different style of delivery, but the same message. We were instructed on how to atone for our past behaviors, particularly our relationship to and with Black women, our families, our communities, and ourselves.

It was stated that we should move toward a more independent economy; unite to restore our communities from the drugs and crime that plague our homes and families; and continue to use our political power to change the interest of our future. It was mentioned that businesses are investing in prisons instead of investing in our culture as a resource. We also learned that the very ground on which we stood was used as an auction block to sell our forebears.

One speaker noted that "God has been with us as a people through all our trials and tribulations and is still with us today." These words were moving. Just like the other 999,999 people who attended the March, I felt I needed to take this information home with me.

Maya Angelou read a poem that she wrote for this occasion. Rev. Jesse Jackson spoke, even though he faced criticism for doing so.

Other speakers included Stevie Wonder, politicians, and ministers from various churches. The list went on and on. This was truly a historic event because it gave people hope.

The final speaker was the March's organizer, Minister Louis Farrakhan. I'm sure everyone will agree that all the speakers of the day were powerful and impressive, but you could tell that everyone was preparing for the main speaker.

Television and radio crews began mike checks. The lighting was checked and rechecked. It was obvious that the media did not want to miss a single word from this controversial speaker. Minister Farrakhan took center stage. His usual harsh, cynical, and sometimes bitter words were different this time. It seemed as though he put his own personal differences aside to deliver a message of peace, unity, and reconciliation for past mistakes, and for men to atone for those mistakes. Even Minister Farrakhan admitted that to bring this many Black men from all parts of the country was not his doing, but rather God's.

I felt totally fulfilled at the close of the day. I thought about civil rights movements and marches from the past. The leaders during that time in history also had unparalleled drive and motivation.

I felt a tremendous sense of recommitment to myself, my family, my community, and to society. I truly believe this experience was an education for everyone who attended, as well as for those who listened on the radio or watched on television.

When I speak of atonement, I believe, as a people, we must have some accountability to our race. We have to start to make personal changes in our behavior and conduct, in our speech, and in our way of thinking. We have to begin to break down the barriers that prevent us from truly becoming the proud nation that we can be.

After all, what good is a powerful national defense if our neighborhoods and communities are deteriorating? Poverty, crime, and racism are some of the major issues we face today. We can only become strong if we attack each issue as brothers joined together. Then, and only then, will we receive the blessings that God has afforded to all humankind.

Symbol to Substance:
Where Do We Go from Here?

MONTE E. NORWOOD

"Long live the spirit of the Million Man March! Long live the spirit of the Million Man March!! Long live the spirit of the Million Man March!!!"

So went the chant on October 16, 1995. It was a holy Day of Atonement. A sacred moment in time. "Long live the spirit of the Million Man March." So chanted the voices of one million-plus African American males who gathered on the steps of the Capitol and beyond. The sons, grandsons, and great-grandsons of enslaved Africans. A sea of generations of African progeny. Males of African descent living in America. The seed of those present at the dawn of humanity—now present to atone, to love, and be reconciled with one another.

Why a Day of Atonement? Why now?

For too long, we as African American males have shrugged off personal accountability and collective responsibility. When it comes to engaging in monogamous, respectful, supportive, and nurturing relationships with our sisters, wives, and significant others, we have often fallen short. When it comes to consistently fulfilling the role of being an active and visible "daddy" to our children, and not just a functional biological baby-maker, we often have missed the mark.

There have been too many times when we did not make or take the time to provide paternal nurture and guidance. We have often failed to be the responsible providers and the mitigating moral agents that God intended for us to be. When it comes to a moral pattern of conduct, integrity of self, and honesty in our dealings, we have too often chosen the flawed ways of our own oppressors and dealt unfaithfully with each other.

Why confront our failures now?

There is never any better time than the present for positive action. Past sins have haunted those of us who care, far too long. Guilt

123

is the inability to live in the present with the baggage of the past. In order to move into a better future, now is the time to confront our individual and collective pasts and to make peace with our present. There is no better time than now.

Still, there are broader concerns, consequences, and convictions which necessitated and motivated the assembly and atonement of over one million African American males on October 16, 1995. Words are inadequate vehicles to describe the historical decimation and the contemporary institutionalized oppression of African males in America. From the holocaust legacy of being torn from the Mother-land and the history of overcoming oppression in America, to self-defeating and self-destructive behaviors, the challenges and odds facing African American males are great.

Statistics are grave. The situation, to a large extent, is bleak. The wholesale repeal of affirmative action. The myopia of three-strike laws which threaten to create a race of dead men walking. Gross disparity in sentencing guidelines for European Americans and African Americans. Rising unemployment and underemployment among African American males. A record number of African American males on death row and under the jurisdiction of the American judicial and penal system—a business which has become the number one growth industry in the United States. The devastation of HIV and AIDS—edging out violent homicide as the leading cause of death nationwide of African American men between the ages of twenty-five and forty.

When the statistics are that grave and the situation that bleak, any symbol of hope is a welcome sign. The peaceful and constructive gathering of over a million men from all over this nation on the Capitol Mall and its surrounds was not only miraculous and historic, it was a symbol of hope. No fighting. No fussing. No profanity. No drugs. Just the healing of wounds. The healing of the African American male psyche. The healing of broken bonds. The pride of being a part of something which only God could do.

As one face in the gathering, I joined in prayer with Christians, Muslims, Black Nationalists, Black Hebrews, and men from a variety of socioeconomic backgrounds and religious traditions. I spoke with others. I listened to and with others. I focused attentively. I was inspired. I learned. I was challenged. I wept. I embraced brothers whose names I did not know. I looked with love on the faces of sisters, fathers, sons, uncles, young brothers, and little brothers, toddlers, and baby boys—who all sought to join together in a cosmic and redemptive moment. Together we were redeemed.

Where do we go from here?

The Million Man March afforded over one million men the opportunity to create a sacred space upon which atonement could be made for sins of commission, omission, and disposition. The March was an opportunity to repent for misdeeds, missed opportunities, and negative attitudes and behaviors, to others and to ourselves.

I made the personal commitment to go back home and to love my wife, children, and my extended family of children (those in need of nurture and guidance in my community and church), as never before.

I made the commitment to treat African American women with respect, honor, and dignity. I made the commitment to do more than talk. I must *show* love and not just *talk* love. As an African-centered and spiritually centered African American male, I must live out the meaning of the *nguzo saba* (the seven principles): *umoja* (unity), *kujichagulia* (self-determination), *ujima* (collective work and responsibility), *ujamaa* (cooperative economics), *nia* (purpose), *kuumba* (creativity), and *imani* (faith). I must make peace with self, with family, with community, and with divinity.

Where do we go from here?

In 1955, a young Martin King led a Montgomery bus boycott which led to the Supreme Court decision that outlawed segregated public transportation. In 1963, King led a march in Birmingham and was a part of the well-known March on Washington, August 28, 1963, which led to the Federal Civil Rights Act of 1964. King and others marched, demonstrated, and struggled, not only to achieve a moral victory, but to push for legislative changes. African Americans must unify and emulate this model. We must coalesce our strength and bring to bear our collective resources to achieve objectives that can be obtained and whose successes can be measured. Our protest must have a meaningful purpose.

We must move forward with a holistic and positive agenda that includes solid planning for the future. We must once again link marching with a concrete legislative agenda.

On the Tuesday following the Million Man March, members of the Congressional Black Caucus (CBC) fought for equity in welfare reform. On the Wednesday following the March, members of the CBC fought Medicare cuts to the poor and elderly. On the Thursday following the March, members of the CBC struggled against unfair sentencing guidelines.

These protests went largely without a direct link to the Million Man March. Any future march, protest, or sociopolitical action must be linked to a concrete moral and legislative agenda that improves the plight of humanity in general and persons of color in particular.

There is no more precious time to give to the development of cult personalities or irrelevant conservative theologies. As the range of speakers at the March suggested, our leadership must be broad, diverse, include women, and be as far-reaching as possible.

We must work with anyone wishing to make a difference. As an African American male who serves as a pastor in a local congregation, I will continue to take concrete steps to accomplish this.

"Long live the spirit of the Million Man March!"

Rise into Flight

MORGAN BURTON JR.

On Monday, October 16, 1995, I, along with a group of friends, drove to Washington, D.C. The trip was breathtaking. There were many carloads of men en route on the ten-hour trip. Once we arrived in Washington, we parked in a parking structure full of cars. There were so many cars that there was no way we could have driven to the Capitol.

We walked to the nearest subway, which took us directly into Washington. From the subway, we managed to walk to the Capitol through the large crowd. We stood in amazement. There were men, men, men, and more men. They were young, old, disabled, and gang members. Everywhere you turned were men! We even saw some White men and women in the gathering.

The temperature of the day was a cool sixty degrees. The oneness of spirit was so immense that it didn't matter that there was no place to sit. We were unified in spirit with God.

Finally, as the speakers began, the whole meaning of atonement was expressed by every speech that was given. As I stood there, I was astounded by the sight of so many men who practiced peace rather than war. I felt so good inside and wished that the day would never end.

But the day did come to an end. As we walked away together with our hearts filled with pride, I wondered, "What now?" I thought that as a race of people we must first *believe in ourselves* in order to succeed. When you believe in something that you think is right, you build self-esteem and rise into flight. If you believe in nothing, you lose touch with your dream and miss the chance to prepare. But when you believe in yourself, find reasons to care, and take hold of your dream, you rise into flight!

The Day We Witnessed Our Potential

CRAIG A. THOMPSON

The word that lingered in my mind throughout my time at the Million Man March was "potential!" What I and many others experienced was a scene that few people, if any, thought they would ever see: Black doctors walking and talking with former gang members; lawyers exchanging ideas with former convicts; elders with gray hair sharing wisdom with young boys with dreadlocks; men who owned businesses listening to the thoughts and reflections of men who had not worked in years. These images were extremely powerful and, at times, slightly overwhelming.

Since the time we have been in the United States, two consistent themes have permeated the minds of African American people: distrust and disunity. Whether externally created or internally cultivated, distrust and disunity have been two key elements related to the thwarting of our potential. Our response generally has been to throw up our hands and say, "We need to get together." We love little catchphrases like "We need unity in the community," and "We need to get together as a people." But in the back of our minds, with no concrete evidence of these events occurring, we still have doubts.

The success of the Million Man March provides us with a blueprint for action. Moreover, it gives us the tangible evidence that we need to make the case for unity in our respective communities. After witnessing and experiencing this monumental event, I can honestly say that I hope that the day of the catchphrase is over!

The question we face at this point is "What now?" How do we take the impact of the March and incorporate it into daily activities? The suggestion that I have for us is the same instruction given to all of the great thinkers, leaders, and even the prophets throughout history: *Read! Read! Read!*

The importance of reading can never be stressed enough. Locked in the pages of books, periodicals, and other publications is information critical to our survival. Those who held our ancestors in bondage locked away information and made it illegal for them to read. The reason was simple: Information plus understanding equals power!

Dr. John Henrick Clarke stated that "Powerful people never teach powerless people how to obtain power." Our ability to take control of our destiny is directly related to the amount and type of information we have about ourselves and the world around us.

It is time for us to make a conscious effort to put the message from the Million Man March into practice. When we see other Black men, do we still look them directly in the eyes and speak? When we witness other Black men committing wrongful acts, do we hold them accountable? When we observe Black men treating Black women disrespectfully, do we "pull their coat"? The actions that were taken at the March are actions that we can apply in our daily lives. Reading and understanding become critical to that process, because the extent to which we are cognizant of the world around us, as well as our roles in it, is the degree to which we do what is necessary to ensure our survival.

If we each take time out of the day to read something enlightening and empowering, we can tap into the strength inherent in all of us. This would make the impact of the Million Man March last and the potential that was exposed there endure. We owe this much to our ancestors.

Strengthening One Generation at a Time

WAYNE L. WILSON

If my people who are called by my name would humble themselves, pray, seek my face, and turn from their wicked ways, then I will hear from heaven, and will forgive their sin and heal their land.

—2 Chronicles 7:14

I didn't know what to expect, but I was going. I didn't know what I was going to do once I got there, but I was going. I didn't know who I was going with, but I was going. I heard what the critics said, but I was going. I was going to the Million Man March! I was going to be One in a Million!

As an adolescent I had read books and viewed videotapes of the historic 1963 March on Washington. The organizers and participants in that March had a cause, a mission, a goal, *a calling.*

On the Friday before the Million Man March, I too felt a calling. And the call was simple: Go to the Mall and be present at the March. It wasn't about who was speaking, who was organizing it, or who was going to be there. It was about unity. It was now time for African American men to stand up and make a point. That point was that we cared about our families and communities and that we were tired of sitting back and watching them erode.

I didn't view the March as having something to prove to the rest of the world. I had no doubt that over a million African American men could get together with one accord in a peaceful manner.

There was some concern about the presence of women on that day, but after a while it became less controversial. As a man who has great appreciation, admiration, love, and respect for my sister and mother, I really didn't think women were being excluded without purpose.

As one who had grown up in the United Church of Christ, I had seen my mother and sister leave home many times to attend women-only conferences. I believe that there are certain times when it is appropriate for men and women to be separated. These are the times when men and women can "let their hair down" and not feel constrained to maintain their egos and/or their special interests.

Most men would not have been any different with a significant number of women in the crowd. However, the Million Man March was designed not for the atonement of the sins of all of God's people, but for African American men. This was significant. It was time for the media to portray African American males in a positive, affirming environment on a national level.

I, along with fellow students and staff, prepared to go to the March at 8 A.M. We met in the lobby of the Howard University School of Divinity. Before we departed, we sang, prayed, and took group pictures to remember the event. One of the moving moments for me was to hear older brothers tell the stories of their experience at the March on Washington. I hadn't been born then, but now I was going to be a part of a march just as significant.

As we walked to the nearest Metro station, we were affirmed by many people who waved at us from their porches and windows and honked their horns. They were with us. The wheel of unity was beginning to turn.

As we approached the Metro station, it was extremely crowded. This was not a problem. Brothers were coming from all over the country: Los Angeles, Phoenix, New York City, Philadelphia, Atlanta. All regions of the country were represented. Brothers who knew how to operate the ticket dispensers were helping those who did not. Men who were not part of a group were invited to join with others. After all, we were all brothers!

The energy level was so high by 9 A.M., I knew that we would succeed in reaching the goal of having over a million men represented. For the first two hours, all I did was stand in the middle of the crowd near the reflecting pool to absorb the spiritual energy that was in the air and enjoy the moment.

We believed that we were a people called by God. Our goal was simple: to come together, pray, seek the face of God, and commit ourselves to turn from our wicked, selfish ways. I really don't know what else people were expecting beyond that. For me, it was enough.

As the afternoon came and the crowd grew a little restless, one brother said to me, "With all of these people out here, you'd think that they'd have us doing something." I looked at him, smiled, and said, "Brother, first of all, you are part of the 'they,' and if you want to do something, do it." I didn't want to do anything specific. I didn't want to perform any tasks. I just wanted to be in the crowd and seize the moment—a moment that will never be repeated.

The March was a call to all African American men. Men who have been on the front lines for years; men who used to be active, but for one reason or another had lost their drive; men who have always neglected their responsibilities for self and others; and young men who are just coming into their own. No matter what segment of America we came from, we knew that beyond the oppression that exists in our communities from external sources, there are the oppressive acts that we, ourselves, commit. We have control over this.

The March was just a first step in turning this thing around. The consensus, I gather, is that we not only *want* to keep moving forward, but we *have* to keep moving forward. I once saw a billboard in Los Angeles that read in bold letters "Give Five." The caption explained that all people should be willing to give 5 percent of their income and 5 percent of their time to activities and organizations that promote human development.

To do this, we do not need more new organizations that feed the egos of their organizers. The church, the NAACP, the Urban League, the SCLC, the fraternities and sororities have always been the guardians of the African American diaspora and already have basic skeletal structures. Some of them may need new leadership, others a new mission statement. We cannot afford to throw the baby out with the bath water.

However, our goal now is to nurture, encourage, and build up the babies of our time so that ten years from now, they too will be ready, willing, and able to "Give Five." The development of the African American community is a long-term goal. Events like the March are simply milestones along the journey. By strengthening ourselves one generation at a time, our future in this realm is looking brighter and brighter each day.

The Million Man March: A Sermon for Discussion

FRANK A. THOMAS

We keep blaming the White man for our problems. Does the White man make a Black man slap a Black woman? Does the White man make a grown Black man slip into the bedroom of a teenage girl?

I asked these questions in an address at a Chicago rally, one week before the Million Man March. I was asked to speak and inspire the already convinced Monday night gathering.

I decided to give some explanation and justification as to why I supported the March in theory and in practice, why I was going to attend with my father, brother, son, nephew, and best friend. These questions summed up the meaning of the entire address and were the foundation of why I felt so compelled to be in Washington.

Many African American families, and indeed many families all over the land, seem to be falling apart. Relationships are the center of family life, and throughout the nation, relationships are in extreme disrepair. If the network and nexus of relationships fall apart, then the family falls apart. I recently read a report from the Council on Families in America. The report, entitled "Marriage in America," said:

> Relationships between men and women are not getting better; by many measures, they are getting worse. They are becoming more difficult, fragile, and unhappy. Too many women are experiencing chronic economic insecurity. Too many men are isolated and estranged from their children. Too many people are lonely and unconnected. Too many children are angry, sad, and neglected.

It is difficult for us to face the fact that the relational network of many families is falling apart.

133

The most critical consequence of the family falling apart is that it leads to a failure in rearing children. Can anyone dispute that there is widespread and growing evidence of failure in rearing children? The symptoms related to the lack of child well-being are well documented in our culture, including rates of delinquency, crime, juvenile homicide, drug and alcohol abuse, suicide, and depression, as well as the growing number of children in poverty, teenage pregnancy, etc.

These problems rumble all over our land from the suburbs to the inner city. The lack of child well-being gives evidence of an uneasiness, a malaise, and an evil which produces a deep anxiety that sweeps the land.

The response of some of the White community to this anxiety has been to return to the vision of the 1950s. I am suspicious that underneath the "Republican Revolution" and the "Contract with America" is, at best, the desire to return to the majority-culture vision of America. This vision dominated the American landscape in the forties and fifties, before the "unsettling" of the 1960s.

There is no new vision—a creative and imaginative response to the anxiety of the modern situation—or a new and creative casting of the bedrock principles that shaped the old vision. There is a nostalgic desire, however, to return to the old vision of what America once looked like before 1960.

In the language of Edwin Friedman, much of America seems to suffer from "imaginative gridlock." The imagination of White America is locked by the anxiety of the present moment, and therefore the country is not able to see any new and fresh possibilities. Without any new possibilities, we must return, we must go back to what we imagine was a simpler and less complicated time.

In reactionary response to the major conservative corrective, many African Americans move to a more militant posture. The conservative Republican agenda is viewed as a commitment to increasing racism and White supremacy. Therefore, the only option available is a more militant and nationalistic posture and stance. This sets the context for an almost unparalleled hearing for Minister Louis Farrakhan and the Nation of Islam in the African American community.

In my opinion, there is no other African American leader who could attract upwards of one million men to Washington, D.C.

Whether we agree with Minister Farrakhan or not, whether we supported the March or not, he was able to name something that was profoundly felt by many men who traveled the highways, buses, trains, and planes of this nation to get to the March. I believe that he: (1) provided an analysis and critique of White racism in the face of the conservative agenda that was a release of frustration for some, and (2) offered a vision and solution to the falling apart of the Black family. It was the maturing critique of White racism and the bold vision of calling Black men to atonement, reconciliation, and responsibility that were at the heart of why so many traveled.

Many Christian ministers could not, in good conscience, support the Million Man March based on their disagreement with Minister Farrakhan on several issues. After pointing to some of his racial views, inevitably many would dissent on religious grounds. Many quote the text of 2 Corinthians 6:14–7:1 (NIV):

> Do not be mismatched with unbelievers. For what partnership is there between righteousness and lawlessness? Or what fellowship is there between light and darkness? What agreement does Christ have with Beliar? Or what does a believer share with an unbeliever? What agreement has the temple of God with idols? . . . Let us cleanse ourselves from every defilement of body and of spirit, making holiness perfect in the fear of God.

These ministers retorted that Paul is clearly stating that believers should not get in a double harness with unbelievers. Within this line of thinking, Farrakhan is considered an unbeliever, and the Bible warns against attachments with unbelievers because they do not share the Christian's standards, sympathies, or goals.

But, in the deepest sense of the text, Paul is suggesting to the Christian: *Do not form any relationship with unbelievers that would lead to a compromise of Christian standards or jeopardize the consistency of the Christian witness.*

I have productively modulated my rage and bitterness at racism in America and did not go to Washington to release my frustration.

I did not go to Washington to play victim and blame White people for all of our problems. I stood on the Capitol Mall at the Million Man March in response to a new vision that was stirring in my heart.

About two years ago, I saw some new possibilities with what I heard articulated as part of the platform of the March. The vision that I saw has three distinct components designed to handle the anxiety of our time: personal responsibility, biblical reconciliation, and the concept of the manly man.

Personal Responsibility

What if we could move past blaming White people for our problems? What if we took personal responsibility for our condition? What if we looked inside our homes instead of looking out to the nation? What if we could take responsibility as men for much of the violence that we perpetrate in our homes? What if we could finally admit that the White man does not make us slap a Black woman? What if we took responsibility for the fact that our problems begin in the relational network of our families?

Biblical Reconciliation

If we could take personal responsibility for our part in our condition, then we could move to biblical reconciliation. Reconciliation from the Christian perspective is not some polite ignoring or reduction of hostility, but rather it is total and objective removal of hostility based on the atonement of Christ. Because God reconciled us in Christ, we are to be ministers of reconciliation to others.

The Manly Man

If we could join personal responsibility with reconciliation, we could model what it means to be a real man—a manly man. A manly man has four virtues:

1. *He bows his knee before God*: A man without God is his own god. A man that is his own god is like a seed blowing in the wind. There is no telling where he is going to land.

2. *He respects the dignity of the female*: We build Black men by respecting the dignity of the female. The more we respect women, the more manly we become. I can only be fully male

if she is fully female. The more I respect, love, and celebrate her, the more manly I become. To diminish her femaleness is to diminish my maleness.

3. *He is vulnerable to the significant people in his life*: The manly man does not play superman, as if life does not hurt sometimes. The manly man is not afraid to show that he does not know everything and understand everything. He is not afraid to admit that he has limits and the fact that life hurts sometimes. A manly man has to cry sometimes.

4. *He is a nurturer*: The manly man does not leave the nurturing, the mentoring, the emotional support necessary to help move others to maturity to women. The manly man provides tenderness, compassion, and understanding which are often necessary for people to mature.

There can never be a revolution in the streets until there is a revolution in the home. Nobody ever will enslave us if our homes are free. The deepest issue is not White racism, but our response.

I understand that racism is an awesome challenge. A challenge is anything that will not change quickly and will take years of strength, effort, and energy to overcome. I understand that our response to challenge is what shapes our character and our destiny. I am trying to live out the values and demands of a vision of personal responsibility, biblical reconciliation, and the manly man.

I believe many who came to the March saw the vision that I saw. Many came to make themselves better fathers, husbands, brothers, uncles, and cousins. Many came to receive empowerment to bless the women and children in their lives. We did not come to curse anyone, but rather to bow our knee to God, to respect the dignity of the female, to admit our human limitations, and become male nurturers.

Amen!

SPEECHES

It's a Brothers' Thing

CONRAD W. WORRILL

Sons of Africa, and to all the daughters of Africa who support this day, and to all the brothers from my hometown, Chicago, and to all the brothers throughout the African world: *As salaam alaikum, habari gani, hotep,* and praise the Lord.

Sons of Africa, as national chairman of the National Black United Front, we bring warm greetings on this holy day—the Day of Atonement, Reconciliation, and Responsibility, the Day of Absence.

We thank Minister Farrakhan for taking on the awesome responsibility in making this call for a million Black men—men of Africa—to march on Washington.

As participants in the worldwide African Liberation Movement, we understand the critical need for Black men to assume greater responsibility in meeting the challenges we face as we enter the twenty-first century.

We must continue to support those Black movement organizations that emerged out of the 1960s, who assumed responsibility for fighting for African independence and freedom, and who are still active participants in the Black Liberation Movement.

We must continue to support the work the Republic of New Africa (RNA) assumed responsibility for, and particularly its leadership, in organizing the National Coalition of Blacks for Reparations in America (NCOBRIA). Thank you, Dr. Imari Obadele and your wife Johnita, for your tireless efforts in assuming responsibility in leading the reparations movement. In this regard, we must continue to assume responsibility for supporting the Conyers Reparations Bill. We demand reparation now!

We must continue to support organizations under the leadership of Chokwe Lumumba which have assumed responsibility for participating in the movement to free all political prisoners like Mumia Abu-Jamal, Geronimo Pratt, Sundiata Acoli, and many, many others.

We must continue to support the work of the All African Peoples Revolutionary Party (AAPRP) and their leader, Kwame Touré, who has assumed responsibility for many years in the struggle to fight for a free and independent Africa that is united and free of European domination.

We in the National Black United Front (NBUF), on this holy day, want you to assume responsibility and join with us in helping to build the African Centered Education Movement, aimed at teaching the truth about African people in the schools of America at all grade levels. We should accept no more untruths about our great history as a people.

Finally, Black men should rededicate themselves and assume greater responsibility for determining our political and economic direction as a people. We must control the economics and politics of our communities.

We should be prepared and assume responsibility to no longer accept the people outside of the African community in America directing, dictating, and controlling what goes on in our communities.

No longer should we be pawns, victims, and subjects of other people's desires. Let us as Black men—African men—assume responsibility for struggling for Black solidarity, justice, freedom, and independence.

May our ancestors bless us always as we prepare to continue to use the spirit of this day to join in partnerships with Black women to help solve many of the problems we face as a people. Let's continue to organize by joining an organization that is fighting for African people. As we said when we marched in by the thousands today: It's a brothers' thing, and we are going to work it out. It's a brothers' thing, and we are going to work it out . . .

Greetings

ROSA PARKS

I honor my late husband, Raymond Parks; other freedom fighters; and men of goodwill who could not be here. I am also honored that young men respect me and have invited me as an elder.

Raymond, or Parks as I called him, was an activist in the Scottsboro Boys case, voter registration, and a role model for youth. As a self-taught businessman, he provided for his family, and he loved and respected me.

Parks would have stood proud and tall to see so many of our men uniting for atonement and committing their lives to a better future for themselves, their families, and this country.

Although criticism and controversy [of the March] have been [the] focus of the media, instead of the benefits of one million men assembling peacefully for spiritual food and direction, it is a success.

I pray that my multiracial and international friends will view this gathering as an opportunity for men—primarily men of African heritage—to make changes in their lives for the better.

I am proud of all groups of people who feel connected to me in any way, and I will always work for human rights for all people. However, as an African American woman, I am proud and applaud and support our men for this assemblage.

Thank you! God bless you all!

Up, You Mighty People

QUEEN MOTHER MOORE

My sons and grandsons, I am your mother and your grandmother in the liberation struggle of all Afrikan people. I am ninety-seven years old and I have been in the struggle for all of my people for seventy-five years.

Struggle is my life. I call on you, my sons, to ask God's forgiveness and the forgiveness of each other, to bond in love for each other, and to unify a force that will mend and heal our broken families.

I was born in a world full of bigotry and hate. A world that raped, lynched, and murdered the spirit and body of many Black men, women, and children.

My sons, I ask that you remember reparations! Over 400 million-plus Afrikans died in the Middle Passage. The greatest holocaust is the African Holocaust. My sons, you must fight for your human rights and your dignity.

My sons, I found you and a great one that I love so dear. I found refuge, strength, and comfort in the loving arms of the Black man called the "Black Moses," the honorable Marcus Mosiah Garvey.

My sons, bond together, straighten out your backs. Up, you mighty people! You can conquer what you will. Up, you Black men. You can conquer.

One God, one aim, and one destiny. God bless you, my sons and grandsons.

Your Afrikan mother

RESOURCES

This resource list represents a selection of organizations that work directly with the needs of African Americans. We strongly suggest that you contact one or more for additional information. There are also many local organizations within your own community that you can contact.

Big Brothers and Big Sisters
  of America
230 North 13th Street
Philadelphia PA 19107
(215) 567-7000

Boys and Girls Club of America
1230 West Peachtree St., NW
Atlanta GA 30309-3447
(404) 815-5700

Concerned Black Men, Inc.
7200 North 21st Street
Philadelphia PA 19138
(215) 276-2260

Congress of National Black
  Churches
Suite 750
1225 I Street, Northwest
Washington DC 20005
(202) 371-1091

Institute for Black Parenting
9920 La Cienega Boulevard
Inglewood CA 90301
(310) 348-1400; (800) 367-8858

The Mentoring Center
Suite 100
1221 Preservation Parkway
Oakland CA 94612
(510) 891-0427

Midnight Basketball Leagues,
  Inc.
3628 Cousins Drive
Springdale MD 20774
(301) 772-1711

My Brother's Keeper
221 Morrill Hall
Michigan State University
East Lansing MI 48824-1936
(517) 353-9252

NAACP
4805 Mount Hope Drive
Baltimore MD 21215
(410) 358-8900

National Black United Front
700 East Oakwood Boulevard
Chicago IL 60653
(312) 268-7500

National Black Youth Leadership
 Council
Mr. Dennis Watson
250 West 54th Street
New York NY 10019
(212) 541-7600

National Council of African
 American Men, Inc.
c/o University of Kansas Center
 for Multicultural Leadership
 Development and Research
1028 Dole Center
Lawrence KS 66045
(913) 864-3990

National Institute for Responsible
 Fatherhood and Family
 Revitalization
8555 Hough Avenue
Cleveland OH 44104
(216) 791-9378

National Urban League, Inc.
500 East 62nd Street
New York NY 10021
(212) 310-9000

Ohio Commission on African
 American Males
340 East Broad Street
Columbus OH 43215
(614) 644-5143

100 Black Men of America, Inc.
Suite 704
127 Peachtree Street, Northeast
Atlanta GA 30303
(404) 525-7111

Operation PUSH
930 East 50th Street
Chicago IL 60615
(312) 373-3366

Project 2000, Inc.
Center for Educating African
 American Males
411 Eighth Street, Southeast
Washington DC 20003
(202) 543-2309

RAISE, Inc.
605 North Eutaw Street
Baltimore MD 21201
(410) 685-8316

The Rosa and Raymond Parks
 Institute for Self Development
65 Cadillac Square
Suite 3200
Detroit MI 48226
(313) 965-0606

Save Our Sons and Daughters
2441 West Grand Boulevard
Detroit MI 48208
(313) 361-5200

CONTRIBUTORS

Steve H. Alexander is married and the father of three sons. He is the vice-president of the Million Man Club, president of Alexander Telecom, and head of Church Ministry to the Incarcerated of Frederick County, Maryland.

Morris Allen Jr. is a husband and the father of one son. He is the president of MAJA Enterprises, his own company.

Shawn M. Barney is a 1996 graduate of Howard University. He was the 1995–1996 president of the Howard University Student Association (HUSA).

Ronald S. Bonner Sr. is the father of two sons. He is the affirmative action officer of the United Church of Christ in Cleveland, Ohio.

Keith Boykin is executive director of the National Black Gay and Lesbian Leadership Forum and author of the forthcoming book *One More River to Cross: Black and Gay in America,* to be published by Doubleday.

Hugh Brandon is a native Chicagoan and an active member of Trinity United Church of Christ.

Howard B. Brookins Sr. is a devoted father and husband. A retired state senator for the 18th Legislative District, he also served two terms in the Illinois House of Representatives. Mr. Brookins is the owner and operator of Brookins Funeral Home in Chicago, Illinois.

Howard B. Brookins Jr. is an attorney living in Chicago.

Neil James Bullock is a mechanical engineer. He is the president and chairperson of the board of directors of Bethel Lutheran Church in Chicago, Illinois. He is also on the Lutheran Human Relations Association in Milwaukee, Wisconsin.

Rev. Dr. Richard M. Bundy Jr. is an associate pastor at New Faith Baptist Church in Matteson, Illinois.

Paul S. Burley is the president of Panorama Advertising, located in Washington, D.C. He was born and raised in Harlem, N.Y.

Morgan Burton Jr. is married and resides in Detroit, Michigan.

Larry Grant Coleman, Ph.D., is an educator, a professional storyteller, and an independent consulting and training services specialist. He works with educational and business clients in the areas of communication, motivation, performance management, and diversity. He currently works as a facilitator for the Efficacy Institute of Lexington, Massachusetts.

Ronald Cook is an office manager for the Convent Avenue Baptist Church in Harlem, N.Y. He is married to the Rev. Dr. Suzan D. Johnson Cook, with whom he has two sons. Ronald also has three other children.

Austin J. Dunn Jr., husband, father, friend, American.

Rev. Dr. Rodney Franklin is a native of Chicago, Illinois. He is currently pastor of First Congregational Church in Birmingham, Alabama. Rev. Franklin was born on October sixteenth.

David P. Gardner, a native New Yorker, is a member of Xi Phi Chapter, Omega Psi Phi Fraternity, Inc. A graduate of Morgan State University, he is currently a vice-president at Americorp Securities, a Wall Street brokerage firm. He is married and the father of one child.

Lawrence Oliver Hall resides in Philadelphia. He is married and the father of two children.

Carl K. Harmon is a managing partner for Harmon Holding Enterprise. He is president of the Cleveland chapter of the National Black MBA Association.

Eric L. Hill is a husband and the father of two daughters. He has a bachelor of science in management from Dyke College in Cleveland, Ohio, and is employed as a claims representative for American States Insurance.

Ben Holbert is a news anchor and reporter for WOIO-CBS/WUAB-TV in Cleveland, Ohio. He started his broadcasting career in 1980.

Jawanza Kunjufu, Ph.D., is a lecturer and consultant, and the author of sixteen books including the best-seller *Countering the Conspiracy to Destroy Black Boys; Adam, Where Are You?;* and *Restoring the Village: Solutions for the Black Family.*

Todd L. Ledbetter is a musician and trainer living in Washington, D.C. He holds a B.A. in communications from the University of Pittsburgh and is president of TTB/KUUMBA Communications.

Douglas S. Lee is a 1996 graduate of Shaker Heights High School in Shaker Heights, Ohio. His reflection won the first-place prize in the Martin Luther King Oratorical Contest, sponsored by Eastview Congregational United Church of Christ.

Cleo Manago is the executive director of the AMASSI Center of South Central, Los Angeles. He is a Black same-gender-loving man.

The Honorable Nathaniel Martin is a councilman for the city of East Cleveland. The father of three children, he is the president of the Men's Fellowship Association of the Euclid Avenue Congregational Church and the president of Kappa Alpha Psi Management Corporation, Cleveland Alumni Chapter.

David B. Miller, Ph.D., is an assistant professor of social work in the Mandel School of Applied Social Science at Case Western Reserve University. He is currently conducting research into the resiliency of African American adolescents.

Dr. Lawrence E. Miller is the third national executive director of Phi Beta Sigma since its founding in 1914 at Howard University. He serves as the chief operating officer for the fraternity's national headquarters in Washington, D.C.

Queen Mother Moore is a civil rights activist.

Silas Norman Jr., M.D., is a physician living in Detroit, Michigan.

Rev. Dr. Monte E. Norwood, a native of Atlanta, Georgia, lectures and preaches in the area of African American religion and culture. The senior pastor of the Imani United Church of Christ in Euclid, Ohio, he is married and the father of three children.

Amoti Nyabongo is a police officer living in Brooklyn, New York. He is a member of Omega Psi Phi Fraternity, Inc.

Rosa Parks is the mother of the civil rights movement.

Wardell J. Payne, Ph.D., is the research director of the Howard University School of Religion, Research Center on Black Religious Bodies. He is also the editor of the *Directory of African American Religious Bodies.*

Rev. Dr. F. Allison Phillips pastored for twenty-three years. He is currently the general secretary of the American Missionary Association of the United Church Board for Homeland Ministries, United Church of Christ.

Wendell Harrison Fitzgerald Phillips is the public relations manager of the Wendell H. Phillips Foundation, Inc., and sales supervisor for a major corporation.

Alex Pickens Jr., M.D., is a physician and the father of two sons who also attended the March. He is happily married to the former Patricia McCollum and resides in Detroit, Michigan.

Alex Pickens III completed his undergraduate studies in May 1996. He will serve a two-year stint with the Peace Corps in West Africa.

Seth Watson Pickens is a first-year honor student at Morehouse College. He plans to become a doctor.

Nathan Warren Reed was the salutatorian of his eighth-grade graduating class. Now fifteen, he is an honor student at Whitney Young Magnet School in Chicago, Illinois. He enjoys reading, working on computers, and playing sports.

James Raymond Reid Jr., a Clevelander, was born in Harlem, N.Y., and attended Salve Regina College in Newport, Rhode Island. Very active in his community, he is the founder and organizer of the Glenville Hoop It Up Summer Basketball Tournament, a program serving over one thousand youth and adults. He dedicates his reflection to his father, the late James R. Reid Sr.

Richard A. Rowe is a father, a husband, and the chief operating officer of RAISE, Inc., a mentoring program designed to enhance the life chances and life options of African American males. He is also the host of a popular weekly radio program, "Dialogue with the African American Male," which airs on Morgan State University's radio station (88.9 FM) in Baltimore, Maryland.

Martini Shaw is an Episcopal priest living in Chicago, Illinois.

Rev. Dr. Jack Sullivan Jr. is the pastor of United Christian Church in Detroit, Michigan.

Rev. Dr. Frank Thomas is the pastor of New Faith Baptist Church in Matteson, Illinois.

Craig A. Thompson is an attorney with the Minority Business Enterprise Legal Defense and Education Fund in Washington, D.C. He also lectures and conducts workshops on the importance of self-esteem and leadership.

André Tramble is an accountant. He is married to a talented and successful woman, and is the father of two lovely, bright children.

Granville K. White is a two-year veteran of the Cleveland Fire Department. Married for eleven years and the father of a son and a daughter, he has been involved in the struggle for the liberation of Black people for the past fifteen years.

Wayne L. Wilson, a resident of Los Angeles, recently completed his last year of studies at Howard University Divinity School. He is a member of the Executive Council of the United Church Board for Homeland Ministries of the United Church of Christ and a member of Pilgrim Congregational Church in Los Angeles.

Conrad W. Worrill, Ph.D., is the national chairman of the National Black United Front (NBUF), in Chicago, Illinois. He is currently a professor and the chairman of the Department of Inner City Studies Education at Northeastern Illinois University.

Thomas E. Wortham III, a native Chicagoan, is a husband and the father of two daughters and one son. A sergeant in the Chicago Police Department, he had the honor of serving on the late Mayor Harold Washington's security team. He is a board member of the African American Police League, a member of the National Black Police Association, and a member of Trinity United Church of Christ. His son, Thomas IV, attended the March with him.

Dr. Jeremiah A. Wright Jr. is the pastor of Trinity United Church of Christ in Chicago, Illinois. He is a professor at United Theological Seminary and Chicago Theological Seminary. Pastor Wright attended the March with his son, Nathan Reed.